Fashion in Film

Fashion in Film

Edited by

Regine and Peter W. Engelmeier

With essays by

Peter W. Engelmeier, Audrey Hepburn,
Melanie Hillmer, Ponkie, Angelika Berg,
and Regine Engelmeier

Prestel

Munich · New York

This book originally accompanied the exhibition *Film und Mode — Mode im Film*
held at the Deutsches Filmmuseum, Frankfurt am Main, Germany, from March 2 to April 1, 1990.
Exhibition concept: Regine Engelmeier.

Revised and updated edition, 1997

Library of Congress Cataloging-in-publication Data
Film und Mode, Mode im Film: English
Fashion in film / edited by Regine und Peter W. Engelmeier; with
essays by Peter W. Engelmeier... [et al]: English translation by
Eileen Martin; edited by Barbara Einzig
p. cm.
Include Index
ISBN 3-7913-1808-x (pbk.)
1. Costume. 2. Costume design. 3. Fashion in motion pictures.
I. Engelmeier, Regine. II. Engelmeier, Peter W. III. Einzig,
Barbara. IV. Title.
PN 1995.9.C56F5513 1997
791.43'026--DC21

Prestel-Verlag · Mandlstr. 26 · 80802 Munich, Germany
Tel. (89) 381 70 9-0; Fax (89) 38 17 09-35
and 16 East 22nd Street, New York, NY 10010, USA
Tel. (2 12) 3 27 81 99; Fax (2 12) 9 27 98 66

Prestel books are available worldwide. Please contact your nearest bookseller or write to
either of the above addresses for information concerning your local distributor.

Cover design by Susanne Rüber, Munich

Front cover (from left to right and top to bottom):
James Dean (illus. 82), Audrey Hepburn (illus. 327), Winona Ryder (illus. 357), Marlene Dietrich (illus. 24),
Edith Head's "Oscars" (illus. 295), Mia Farrow and Robert Redford (illus. 80),
Marcello Mastroianni and Sophia Loren (illus. 59), Terence Stamp (illus. 359), Brigitte Bardot (illus. 53),
Gary Cooper, Claudette Colbert, Ernst Lubitsch (illus. 14)

Back cover (from left to right and top to bottom):
Marlene Dietrich (illus. 264), Eddie Murphy (illus. 256), Jean-Paul Belmondo and Jean Seberg (illus. 245),
Faye Dunaway and Warren Beatty (illus. 88), Wu Chun Mei (illus. 352), Kevin Costner (illus. 254),
scene from *Mad Max 2 – The Road Warrior* (illus. 253), Mark Hamill, Harrison Ford and Carrie Fisher (illus. 342),
Greta Garbo (illus. 259), Michelle Pfeiffer and John Malkovich (illus. 353), Madonna (illus. 70)

The endpapers feature a scene from *Bedtime Story*, 1942,
with Loretta Young and Fredric March; Stanley Brown and Robert Benchley
are eyeing them from their seats.

Frontispiece: Marlene Dietrich in *The Flame Of New Orleans*, 1941

(Photos from the Peter W. Engelmeier Filmhistorisches Bildarchiv, Munich)

English Translation by Eileen Martin, edited by Barbara Einzig

Designed by Heinz Ross, Munich

Printed in Germany

ISBN 3-7913-1808-X

Printed on acid-free paper

Contents

Acknowledgements

The editors particularly wish to thank their colleagues and staff: Swantje Thomae, Angelika Berg, Hans W. Fink, Sabine Pichlau, Heide Müller, Antje Reincke, and all the photo-editorial staff of the pwe-Verlag, Munich, who have also been responsible for conservation work on Peter W. Engelmeier's collection.

Our warm thanks also go to Walter Schobert and Jürgen Berger of the Deutsches Filmmuseum' who gave the exhibition prominence in their fine building in Frankfurt. Peter Hoenisch of RTLplus (television) opened the way for future exhibitions.

We also wish to thank Leendert de Jong of the Filmstichting Den Haag, who was ever willing to help with answers to many questions and always ready to offer friendly advice. We received welcome suggestions from Marian Conrads, head of the fashion department of the Koninklijke Academie van Beeldende Kunsten in Den Haag and Ietse Meij, curator at the Kollektion Nederlands Kostuummuseum in Den Haag.

Unfortunately, it is possible neither to provide a complete list of the sources of our illustrations nor to give the names of all the photographers. Many traces are now lost, particularly for the older pictures. Many of the photographs are from the former Goepfert archives in Lugano, Switzerland, which had an international reputation. The stills were made for the films in question and then released. Wim Wenders's Road Movies GmbH provided the photo for the Yamamoto film, and the photo from Peter Greenaway's film *The Cook, the Thief, His Wife and Her Lover* came from Pandis/Sygma.

Our thanks also go to the producers and distributors who have helped to make our collection such an extensive and well-known one; these include United Artists, Paramount, Metro-Goldwyn-Mayer, Warner Brothers, Columbia Pictures, UIP, Fox, Jugendfilm, Senator, Scotia, Futura, endfilm, Kinowelt, and many others all over the world.

Doris Kutschbach has our grateful thanks for her careful scrutiny of the final version of the text.

Finally, we wish to thank Prestel-Verlag, Munich, for making this catalogue available to the English-speaking public.

Regine and Peter W. Engelmeier

A Touch of Mink

Film and Fashion – Fashion in Film

A split second, a single glimpse can create a passion for a certain look: once, in the darkness of a movie theater, someone is fascinated by the dress, the presence of a figure on the screen. From that moment, they are driven to make that image their own. It's the start of a trend.

It is impossible to gauge just how often a film star, by appearing in a particular dress or suit, or perhaps only through the use of an accessory, hairstyle, or a detail of makeup, can provoke millions of imitations and thus create a fad. There is, however, no question that fashions would be far less influential without the medium of cinema; the work of couturiers and costume designers would be far less effective without those marvelously casual, tough, delicate, cool beautiful people whom they have to dress — and who in turn inspire their contemporaries.

In these photos, ranging from the early days of the cinema to the present, the stars and starlets reveal to us the intimate connection between fashion and the movies. They pose and improvise under the studio lights, and we can almost hear the rustle of taffeta and feel the smoothness of a touch of mink.

We have always known that such photographic documentation was of great potential, and we have worked long and hard to build a collection with such a wealth of material that we simply could no longer keep it to ourselves. Our original exhibition, *Film und Mode — Mode im Film,* was exhibited in 1989 at the Munich Film Festival by director Eberhard Hauff, attracting forty thousand visitors. We soon learned of other venues — the Deutsches Filmmuseum Frankfurt/Main, for instance, under Walter Schobert, and later the Museum für Angewandte Kunst in Cologne. The present volume is our response to the many enquiries by exhibition visitors, and it contains the essential elements of this popular exhibition.

We have always emphasized the very personal nature of our selection. The exhibition features nearly five hundred photographs, a dazzling array that was also of great value to the specialists among our visitors. The photographs displayed in the exhibition and in this book represent a careful selection from our collection of over one million photographs. We have chosen those which in our view express best the collection's themes; most show the stars of the dream factory in glamorous poses. The group as a whole makes evident the powerful influence of Hollywood, which has drawn many designers into its creative wake. The quality of the stills also played a part in the selection, eliminating most examples from German films after the 1960s.*

All photographs included come from our collection, and after extensive research we have included information on the costume designers (see the Catalogue Checklist). We should like to expressly mention that this is the first publication to

---

* A separate publication will soon be devoted to German costume designers.

provide a complete list of all the films that have been awarded an Oscar for Costume Design.

Many of the photographs, especially those from the brilliant chroniclers of the great studios in Hollywood, have a charm that is often hard to explain, drawing us to linger over them and to study them intensely. As the German still photographer Lars Looschen stated in 1972: 'I have an unshakable faith in the language of photography, and when I work with actors I not only create a document of a situation but also transmit a feeling — there is a language awakened by photographs, so to speak, a language that everyone understands, although they cannot speak it.'

When we gaze in admiration and astonishment at the photographs in our collection (and we still do, over and over again!), when we let them take us back to the glamorous age of the movies, we always feel that a past is reawakened, evoked by these unique personalities. Stories rise up from the depths of the archives, and an incredible range of creative work and achievement is recalled. We experience lives, plots, happy endings. We feel our way around the silken material from which the Big Time was cut.

As the photos are taken up and laid down again, our fashion show is a revival of the strangest figures and of encounters of the most abstruse kind.

It also brings moments of happiness when one stumbles on tracks that had seemed to be already covered by the dust of history or blown away, gone with the wind. 'All these beautiful photographs could keep me awake at night,' as Anne Volk, chief editor of the magazine *Brigitte,* once said, while looking at yellowing stills of Cary Grant. Uschi Power, head of our archives, still exclaims, although she has been handling the finest for years: 'Isn't it a dream? It's from another world.' Sometimes she means the photo as a photo. But often she is speaking of the language that Looschen has defined with such self-confidence, the imagination of the soul of the camera.

Film is the art of myriad and wonderful illusions. Fashion is 'the play of demand and deviation, of craving and calm, of submission and defiance' (Beate Wedekind in an *Elle* editorial in February 1990). Through this dialectic a symbiosis is created. The myths enacted in the movies become visible within the fixed frame of the photograph. The consequences for fashion are clear: millions will wear what they see there. When we gaze at the movie stars in this book, at their remote beauty, we experience for a moment the dependence of film on fashion and of fashion on film. They, and the theme they evoke, are exciting, fascinating, vain — above all, immortal.

Audrey Hepburn

The Costumes Make the Actors

A Personal View

The costume designer does much to characterize a film, for he decides what each individual figure in it will look like. So the success of a production depends to quite a large extent on his work. The costume designer has a great task and great responsibility: he has to be not only a creative artist but often a historian, a researcher, and a craftsman all in one.

When I was under contract to Paramount in Hollywood, Edith Head, winner of many Oscars for Costume Design, was in charge of the studio's costume department.

In *Sabrina*, my second film for Paramount, I played the daughter of a chauffeur, who is sent to Paris to do a cookery course. When she returns home, she has become an elegant lady, thanks to French couture.

I suggested that, to make this metamorphosis evident, we could commission a genuine French couturier. Edith Head listened to the proposal —

Audrey Hepburn surrounded by models presenting creations by the French couturier Givenchy, in the Dutch fashion house of Gerzon in 1953

Sabrina, 1954

and in private life. I have often been asked: Why him particularly? The answer is simple. Apart from his artistic achievements and his talent and specialized knowledge, I have always been impressed by his modesty, his angelic patience, and his humor. His taste always harmonized with mine.

His marvelously sure sense of color put life on the screen. His red coats, apple-green costumes, or the dress in shocking pink have never been forgotten by cinemagoers, nor has the delicate lace creation I wore when I sailed down the river with Fred Astaire in *Funny Face.* And Givenchy's hats! They always made the face appear in close-ups like a wonderfully framed picture. Givenchy's creations always gave me a sense of security and confidence, and my work went more easily in the knowledge that I looked absolutely right. I felt the same at my private appearances. Givenchy's outfits gave me 'protection' against strange situations and people, because I felt so good in them. In a certain way one can say that Hubert de Givenchy has 'created' me over the years.

and agreed, with her own particular brand of enthusiasm, and from then on she remained modestly in the background.*

My choice fell on Hubert de Givenchy, the youngest and most innovative fashion designer in Paris. He had just aroused great excitement in the fashion world with his new collection and was enjoying a tremendous boom. So I could hardly have chosen a less suitable moment to give him a commission. But although Givenchy was fully occupied with the opening of his new couture house and was working at full pressure on his new autumn and winter collection, he made time for me and my request. That created a friendship between us that is still strong today.

The story is well known. Since then Hubert de Givenchy has always dressed me — professionally

---

* The film was awarded an Oscar for Costume Design, and in her acceptance speech Edith Head was generous enough to point out how much Givenchy had contributed, stating that without his work her success would not have been possible. Audrey Hepburn was nominated for an Oscar for her role. Ed.

War and Peace, 1955

Maria de Matteis, who designed the costumes for *War and Peace,* was also a highly gifted costume designer and a sensitive artist, who understood as much about history and literature as she did her own profession. She created Natassia for me, a complete figure, into whioch I only had to breathe life as an actress.

The costumes I wore in the films *The Unforgiven* and *Bloodline* were particularly important, for the ordinary appearance, the natural effect of clothes that look old and worn is very difficult for a costume designer to achieve. Dorothy Jeakins was very experienced (she was nominated for an Oscar) and could design very credible wardrobes of this kind. She is a genius at handling textiles and colors, and she knows how to make materials look old or faded by the sun. Her sure instinct for the right atmosphere makes her unique in the business.

Of course I must also mention Cecil Beaton here. No one had so extensive a knowledge of the time in which *My Fair Lady* is set as he. He was familiar with all the nuances of fashion of the time, and that is why his costumes for the film were of such unsurpassable elegance. I shall never forget the endlessly long wardrobe rooms at Paramount for that film, packed with all sorts of accessories — feathers, flowers, lace, tulle, coats, hats, and shoes, as far as one could see. Cecil Beaton had accumulated most of this treasure trove from museums, private houses, and secondhand shops.

The Unforgiven, 1960

When I was put into the magnificent black-and-white costume for the Ascot scene, I felt I only needed to look up under my huge hat and speak the fine words by George Bernard Shaw and Alan Jay Lerner…

If clothes maketh man, then costumes certainly make actors and actresses. I have much for which to thank the talented men and women on whom I have always been able to rely.

Melanie Hillmer

The Cinema in the Wardrobe

A Stroll through Seven Decades

Madonna, in *Desperately Seeking Susan,* said that we've seen it all before. And it is true that many of us have a favorite outfit in our wardrobe that has been inspired by a film and worn to help us play our everyday roles. The feather boa and the trench coat, the little black dress and the black leather jacket pass across the movie screen and into the realm of our desires. The clothes worn by immortal stars and long-forgotten starlets serve as a pattern for our dreams and nightmares, and for things of which we have not yet dreamed. When we take clothes out of context, we can slip into the role of Marlene, Humphrey, Audrey, James, speaking their sartorial language with our bodies. We are the copy, the variation, the improvisation, the parody. We love the game — for, to paraphrase Oscar Wilde, it is more real than life.

When the celluloid began to move it was in a world of disorder. Ordinary people lined up at the box offices of movie theaters to see melodramatic and grotesque films, full of rolling eyes and wildly gesticulating hands, to see a world not necessarily attractive, but one that could have been much worse, as the projectionists could show when given the signal. In 1910 it was calculated that in 250 films there were 97 murders, 45 suicides, 51 cases of adultery, 12 seductions, 22 abductions, 25 drunks, and 45 prostitutes. Their destinies were underscored by the pianist playing the thunderstorm from Rossini's *William Tell* overture, or Chopin's Funeral March.

The demands of the plot and the erotic standards of the time required the heroine to have the strength of a Brunhilde but a temperament of angelic sweetness. Her literary models were in Dickens and Poe, while she visually harked back to the Pre-Raphaelite nymphs and to fairytales. Psychologically the audience was still in the corset of Victorianism: they loved the pudgy girl-women in short fluttering organdy dresses, pretty frocks edged with lace and ribbons in the dairy-maid style, with apron and pockets, puff sleeves, and garlands of flowers. Their tiny feet were in buttoned boots, their angelic hair a mass of corkscrew curls. The Lolita of the silent film was Mummy's little girl; she loved small dogs and curt-sied obediently to Mummy's lover. She had that certain something, but something was missing, too. May Pickford, Lillian Gish, Mabel Normand, Blanche Sweet, and Mary Miles Minter took our heroine into new territory; they were the first 'broken blossoms.' We shall meet these 'pretty babies' again, in teddies or hot pants and little slippers, saying silly things in their high voices — they are now called Sue, Nastassia, Jodie, Brooke.

Love, passion, the senses! The vamp came on the scene as Appolonia Chalupec, better known as Pola Negri, stepped before the camera. Of medium height, not particularly slim but very pretty, with black hair and eyes and a Polish temperament, she appeared first in films where lions devoured Christians while old buildings collapsed, and then in a version of Bizet's *Carmen,* a subject, incidentally, that was made ten times in ten years and, as we know, had countless successors. Pola's breakthrough came with the Lubitsch film *Die Augen der Mumie Ma,* made in the Riedersdorf chalk hills near Berlin.

Passion, the American version of the Dubarry story made in 1918 with Emil Jannings, took our heroine to Hollywood and made her a Paramount star. Her costumes in the film and in real life stood out, with pomp and pathos unashamedly linking hands. Caligari cloaks with batwing sleeves, draperies, and bizarre accoutrements were used to exaggerate her erotic, demonic allure in the jungle. Finally it all descended into caricature and the fantastic faded out.

Murmuring that she was made for love from head to toe, the artiste Lola Lola in *The Blue Angel* sang her way into film history in a black dress with silver collar and sleeves:

> Men gather round me
> Like moths around a flame
> And if their wings burn
> I know I'm not to blame …

With Marlene Dietrich the curtain opened, slowly but surely, on the emancipated woman. In lace culottes she blazed the way for the jazz babies of the Roaring Twenties. Girls with bobbed haircuts and little satin slips, à la Louise Brooks and Clara Bow, matched the mood of the big cities to a tee.

The cinema broke with the social conventions of the postwar period, as was evident to any audience as they chewed on their candy. *Don't Change Your Husband* was a successful joke even in the title. Gloria Swanson's perfumed appearance and champagne smiles were predestined for the boudoir comedy. In *Male and Female* she was sent from the world of bubble baths and champagne to a lonely island. But the butler was there, and he became her lover. Whatever Swanson did she always managed to look good. Her luxury was ruinous — her expensive accessories, her legendary evening dresses, her silver foxes degraded to dusters. She was the queen, and her audience got the message.

Our mothers and our grandmothers dropped their corsets and became flappers, slipping into straight, waistless shifts in satin and velvet. They wore close-fitting cloches and headbands and were led across the floors of dance clubs by gentlemen in dinner jackets; some held on tight to Valentino gigolos in wide tango trousers and short jackets. Pearls and fringes swung to the rhythm of the Charleston and the Shimmy, while black-rimmed eyes gazed skeptically into the future. The break-through was a puff of smoke from the obligatory cigarette holder. The tenor sax stopped playing and the easygoing ways ended with the Great Crash of 1929. Hollywood did not make a diagnosis: it just provided the medicine of entertainment.

Joan Crawford declared her belief in the dollar through spending it all; her lips often took on the shape of a diminutive gold bar. She was one of the main figures in the escapist films of the Golden Thirties, forming the great triumvirate at MGM with the charismatic Garbo and the blameless Norma Shearer. Their shoulderpads were the mark of a new idol: the woman who lives her life to the full, the self-made woman. During the day she wore figure-revealing dresses. Hoods and scarves framed the beauty of the face in close-ups. The working girl of the thirties was a lady in a tailored, duotone suit, sometimes double-breasted. The skirt might be pleated or flared, the blouse with a jabot or bow. The emphasis was on the hats, and they were true creations. Price was no object; they were copied by salesgirls, secretaries, the girl next door.

The brilliance of wealth, beauty, and luxury was the silver-plated leitmotiv of Hollywood; money paved the way of the femme fatale. The goddesses of the screen swayed in streamlined backless dresses in satin and lamé, ancient and mythical, at a remove from the mundane world. Asymmetrical low Diana necklines signaled the desire of the huntress. Ocelot and mink were tossed casually over the shoulder as accessories in publicity poses, and the diamond necklace might on occasion fall at the feet of a lover. There were beaded dresses in *Dinner at Eight,* crinolines in *Camille,* and dresses for waltzing in a flood of cinematic operettas and musicals, where the script was only the occasion for a lineup of the sweetest girls in the world, a dynamic frame for them and their elegant partners. Ginger Rogers and Fred Astaire danced their shoes off.

Success typecast the stars. Douglas Fairbanks fought his way through the cloak-and-dagger films as an acrobatic Don Juan. Gary Cooper and James Stewart were heroes of ordinary life, Spencer Tracy the honest man in the underworld. Boris Karloff was a monster, the Marx Brothers absurd characters of slapstick humor, while Vivien Leigh and Clark Gable created the unique experience of *Gone with the Wind,* the epic story of the love of Scarlett O'Hara and Rhett Butler, the downfall of the house of Tara, and the American civil war.

America was looking to history. The Western flourished. 'Broncho Billy' Anderson, cowboy in 376 movies, always said it was better to change horses than to change the subject, and this remark certainly applied to the clothes worn in these films. The problems encountered on the long ride from barbarism to civilization were always solved

Wallace Beery, Jean Harlow in *Dinner at Eight,* 1933

in jeans. They were the symbol of toughness, resistance, and sincerity, for the asphalt cowboys as well.

GIs stuck pin-ups on theirs walls to pass the time until the next leave. Betty Grable, Dorothy Lamour, Hedy Lamarr, and Lana Turner were the favorites in the photographic striptease. They had Sex Appeal: sweaters filled with very evident femininity, teasing hula skirts. Vargas girls were scantily clad in the American flag, bolstering the morale of the front-line troops everywhere with come-hither looks.

Meanwhile the fiancée at home was fighting to make a passable copy within the limitations of wartime rationing. A seam painted on the legs did duty for the unobtainable nylons, if she did not go back into socks. Old things from the thirties were resurrected with wit and invention, and true creations came from the home sewing rooms, complemented by a full perm under hairnet or head scarf. Plastic and bakelite took the place of gold and silver, and instead of leather soles she walked on cork platforms to the movies, where she could choose between losing herself in Tyrone Power's adventures, or diving in with a technicolor Esther Williams.

Humphrey Bogart, alternately surrounded by dubious blondes and beaten up by unfeeling gangsters, reflected the disconcerting experiences of the average American. Jackets were cut wide to take handguns, casual trousers were held up by broad suspenders. The shirt was in a contrast color, tie and pocket handkerchief carefully chosen and striking. Rings and gold chains signaled the wages of fear.

The country needed new women — Lauren, Ava, Rita. Their masculine trappings in no way contradicted their feminine charms, as Rita Hayworth demonstrated in *Gilda.* The blonde manes of Veronica Lake and Lauren Bacall became so popular with working women that the government had to ask Paramount to do something about it to stop further accidents in the factories. Women on the conveyor belts and in the offices identified with the realistic and open ambience that was being projected.

American fashion magazines, intent on ensuring that every consumer find an advertisement to suit her taste, now began to promote specific types of women: the sporty Katherine Hepburn, the exclusive Merle Oberon, the feminine Greer Garson, the exotic Ilona Massey. Women indexed their type and over the years would play their role: flat shoes, sweaters, slacks. Hollywood discovered psychoanalysis. In the sea of neuroses the war was creating, many no longer knew what they were doing. Women who loved too much or not at all were on the verge of a nervous breakdown and, despite a home of their own, a refrigerator, and a record player, they reached out for a bottle of gin.

The children of the lost generation rebelled against the belief in persistence and progress, attacking the family and school with self-destructive zeal. Marlon Brando and James Dean were variations on the antihero in a purist alliance of T-shirt, jeans, and leather jacket, and when Elvis stepped to the microphone and his electric guitar roared out under a few sweeping gestures, the world was ruthlessly divided into the young and the old. Bad boys chewing gum, dressed in black shirts with slicked-back hair, comb ready at hand in their rear pockets, threw screaming teenagers in fondant petticoats over their shoulders. In ice cream parlors as brash as a fairground, the jukebox pounded out the latest hits, while a motorcycle waited outside.

Parallel to the aesthetic of the dreamy teenager — dressed in full skirt, bobby socks, and bright blouse — burned the fuse of the sex bomb. According to the psychologists, her target was man, weaned of the breast and the pacifier, and now in search of the simplest and most natural thing in the world. Blondes were the favorites, and they stumbled into exotic adventures in tightly cut dresses. The 'itsy-bitsy teenie-weenie yellow polka-dot bikini,' not to be confused with the simple maillot of the prewar period, held the pneumatic charms of Jayne Mansfield, the rich pasta-fed outlines of Sophia Loren, and the curves of Marilyn Monroe. The red lamps never went out again. The starlets, mobbed by reporters and photographers at the Cannes film festival and at beauty

Veronica Lake, 1945

contests from Rimini to Borkum, made sure that the two-piece bathing suit got the press it deserved. 'Is my figure good enough for a bikini?' was the most urgent question of the day.

In contrast to the overwhelming aura of the stars who took off their clothes, Audrey Hepburn was an individual event, to be forever associated with her role in *Breakfast at Tiffany's* — the little black dress, elegant accessories, eyes hidden behind huge sunglasses.

'Someone who follows her instincts blindly,' said Roger Vadim of BB. In this case initials are enough to describe a microcosm, a feat only MM was otherwise to achieve. As a French women's magazine proclaimed of Bardot when she appeared in *En cas de malheur*, 'The closer her face, hair, and clothing come to nature, the more powerful is the sensual impression she leaves on those around her.'

The lion's mane, the sulky mouth, and the bare feet were copied not by Madame in the 16th arrondissement but by schoolgirls who moistened their mascara with spit, put on white lipstick, and teased their hair. The sixties showed that mankind is basically an unknown entity. Analytical films attempted to find the answer. Carnaby Street and Kings Road were where it was at; 'kicks' came right off the street, and at a speed that took the commercial fashion world by surprise. The 'looks,' as costuming from head to toe was now called, followed and displaced each other at breathtaking speed, with mini giving way to maxi and the knitted look yielding to the space suit, followed by the Turkish, Indian, Russian, the Mao and the Hippie look, and culminating in a general fraternization of styles that followed Andy Warhol's doctrine — 'Everything's beautiful.'

In *Bonny and Clyde* Faye Dunaway and Warren Beatty shot out an opening for the fashions of Prohibition and the Depression, while *The Great Gatsby* satisfied the longing for beauty. 'I have never seen such beautiful shirts,' says Mia Farrow to Robert Redford when he tosses several dozen to the ceiling in the dressing room of his white villa. In this scene Mia wears a transparent wisp of a dress in lilac, a color ambivalent as the lady herself. Robert's pink suits are startling, but they match the honey-yellow parquet, the grass-green golf course, the lemon-yellow Rolls. In short, the mood of this nostalgic film was created by money or the desire for it.

After signs of exhaustion and in the sobriety of reflection, it was evident that a curious collection of glittering rags had accumulated in the wardrobe, and away from the underground and club scene they seemed out of place or even worn out.

Beneath the motto 'the personal is the political,' a wave of films concerned with consciousness-raising set in; the process was worked out at home in a jogging suit. The second wave of feminism, the new motherhood, the new intensity, awareness of the environment, of the body, coming out — these were the themes that pointed fashion in the direction of gym shoes, sweat shirts, cloth coats.

Rouge et noir – and with the clatter of castanets Carmen entered the stage and revitalized the scene. With Amadeus, the wild young composer at the harpsichord, a *da capo al fine* of the pre-revolutionary outfit set in — *Cosi fan tutte* in Murray F. Abraham's tapestry vests, with lace ruffles

Sigourney Weaver in *Ghostbusters 2,* 1989

and brocade jackets. The intrigues of Glenn Close and John Malkovich put the emphasis on cleavage, and evening wear flirted with the delicate theme of *Dangerous Liaisons.*

Baroness Blixen in *Out of Africa* receives no reply to the question as to whether the light would glitter in a color she had worn. Her lover is dead, his grave watched over by lions, the coffee plantation burnt down. She leaves her farm dressed for town, and in our memories she leaves the image of an emancipated woman in white linen blouses and blue ties, safari hats, jodhpurs, polished boots. Her stories are fantastic journeys without luggage, and there is no happy end.

Jim, in *Desperately Seeking Susan,* says that he cannot imagine Madonna leading an ordinary life, but that is just what attracts him to her. Christian Lacroix outfits her in a green bustier; Karl Lagerfeld groans: 'All my young women at Chanel want to look like the Madonna videos.' Somehow it all comes off, from the toy-boy belt to the pure white lace bustier (*Like a Virgin*), the accessories for the magic act in the red-light district, the androgynous game in leather and Hell's Angel garb, the pro-punk, neo-Marilyn nature girl. Sympathy for the scene is assured: Madonna is the ultimate copy. Jean-Luc Godard says she is often better than the original.

The stars of the eighties appear to be of little interest as vehicles for erotic projection. Filming is hard work, and they perform it with taut nerves, a masochistic passion and knife-sharp precision; the cinema still has one foot in life, but the roles offer no scope at all for myth-building. What did Diane Keaton, Meryl Streep, or Sigourney Weaver actually wear, you ask yourself as you leave the movies. Probably something like what you are wearing yourself.

Angelika Berg and Regine Engelmeier

Design or No Design

Costume Designers and Couturiers in the Great Days of Hollywood

Professionals polished the script. Professionals directed and shot the films. Professionals thought about the sets and adjusted the lighting. Filmmaking, even in the early days, needed careful planning and the input of specialists. But the costumes for the cast were often hand to mouth.

At the beginning of the century, when films had to be taught to walk, and in the first decades of the cinema proper, the great producers liked to improvise. The woman in the cast were often the ones who concerned themselves with the costume requirements of the stage manager – and who solved his problems.

A true story is often told in low-budget filmmaking regarding *Birth of a Nation* (D. W. Griffith, 1915) – Lillian Gish's mother, always an involved and practical woman, designed the costumes at home and sewed them herself (see illustration). Those who did not have a Momma Gish on their team obtained the outfits for the cast from theatrical stores or costume agencies.

As the Roaring Twenties began, professionals were called in for costuming as well. More producers began giving contracts to specialists whose only responsibility was to fulfill the fashion requirements of the cast (and this certainly helped the quality of the moving pictures). By the end of the twenties every studio of rank had its own costume department, with a full-time staff of designers, milliners, tailors, and seamstresses, all of sure and proven taste. The last gap in the team of studio professionals had been filled.

It is astonishing that it took so long, for what people wear and call fashion has always been an important determinant of other people's reaction to them, and this was particularly true for the 'traveling players' – long since renamed actors and actresses. The realization that the public cares about costumes, that critics notice them (and write about them!), marked the start of a new awareness of the long-neglected area of the visual and of creative design in film.

Specialists have repeatedly chosen to write about the great days of costume design in Hollywood. This was the real home of the métier, –

Lillian Gish in 1915
in a homemade costume
for *Birth of a Nation*

where fashion in the movies grew up, where the professionals were discovered and promoted, where the new values became evident. Only since 1948 has there been an Oscar for Costume Design, a very late recognition of a discipline that had long been contributing to the enjoyment of millions of people all over the world as they viewed the productions of the film industry.

There can be no doubt that the makers of heavenly, earthly, or devilish (*The Witches of Eastwick*) clothes have given the trade in illusions an additional dimension. The audience, the critics, the specialists, the imitators, and the collectors of old stills have over the course of time been attracted to and influenced by the achievements of the costume designers.

It is generally acknowledged that French, English, Italian, and German designers were overshadowed by the Hollywood greats, and they still are. This is a fact. Excellent individual achievements have been overlooked, and will continue to be overlooked, lost in the larger picture. The publicity at which Hollywood is supreme promotes the work of the studio's own costume designers or that of the couturier the studio has engaged. European costume designers have really won honors only when they have worked for the great studios of Hollywood.

The image of the idols who entrance millions as they move across the screen is determined to a considerable extent by their costume designers (as well as by the designers who dress them for the glare of publicity offscreen). The difference between the character, the star, and the real person in subject to a retouching process which is scarcely visible; creating the compound identity of the great lady of the cinema, the great star at a gala, and finally the private person, no longer quite so great a lady (because she is not in spike heels and a robe) but still appealing and being appealed to: the autograph is the standard sign of the attraction of the well-dressed screen star.

That actors and actresses may well continue to play their roles in what should be their private lives has much to do with their clothing. We only need think of Marlene Dietrich. Without the work of designer Travis Banton she would not have had that shimmering allure or that provocative style she made so much her own. In the masculine suits that Banton dreamed up for her and her alone, Marlene D. was sure her appearance would be spectacular outside the studio as well. A costume around the clock is a guarantee of unbroken publicity for the superstar.

We can say it again: Hollywood was the centre of the film fashion world and it remained so for a long time. But many European talents helped it to its greatness.

If Hubert de Givenchy had not been so faithful to his beloved Audrey Hepburn, she would not have been so faithful to her type (and to Givenchy) or have had so sure a taste. Perhaps the shy creature she has remained in the memory of millions would have been a little mouse in a rough cloth coat or a neat checked skirt with matching beret, if such may be imagined. On the award of the Golden Globe in 1990 the beautiful Audrey Hepburn, now a hardworking ambassador for UNICEF, appeared before her fans, effortlessly enchanting her international public. Naturally, she wore a dress by Givenchy.

Another Frenchman who made his career in the United States was Jean Louis, whose legendary 'Put the Blame on Mame' dress for the breathtaking Rita Hayworth made film history in *Gilda* of 1946.

'Et Dior créa la femme': the inventive and versatile Christian Dior, with his neurotic concern for his reputation, made sure he seized the chance offered by the growing film industry after the constraints of the war. In 1947 he showed the astounded world his New Look, and Marlene Dietrich was quick to ask the master to work for her. Around 1951 Dior designed the costumes she wore with such success in Alfred Hitchcock's *Stage Fright* and in Henry Koster's *No Highway in the Sky*.

Is it conceivable that the self-confident and narcissistic Monsieur Dior was afraid of Marlene Dietrich and Travis Banton? He was. He kept his designs secret from the great lady right up to the last moment, for fear they might be prematurely revealed to the press or be otherwise prey to indiscretion. He was also afraid of being compared with Dietrich's longtime favorite, Travis Banton. This shows the difference between a couturier and a costume designer very clearly. The couturier creates an ideal image based solely upon his own subjective aesthetic and ideas. His work is initially made for a model of his choice whose body conforms to his notion of ideal measurements. The costume designer on the other hand works to a script and must serve the character in the role and personality they are to represent. Right from the start, he knows the fictive and real persons who will wear his clothes, and his job is to find the proper apparel for them. His task is defined in very concrete terms, in contrast to the relatively abstract work of the couturier, whose wealth of invention is subject to no bounds.

That couturiers nevertheless like to subject themselves to the constraints of film production (and do so) is partly due to the publicity effect of these contracts. A successful film with a big star is the best advertisement. Only recently has a special form of this kind of cooperation between couturier and film studio emerged — 'promo costuming.' It consists of a well-known fashion designer providing the entire costume collection for a film, ready to wear, and this is financially advantageous to the film producer. One recent example of promo costuming is Oscar de la Renta's work for the 1987 'brat pack' film *Bright Lights, Big City* by James Bridges.* There are also cases in the history of cinema where couture failed. In 1931 Coco Chanel was not successful in Hollywood because she clung too closely to the firmly defined style of her house and failed to recognize a new fashion trend in time. Her costumes for Gloria Swanson in *Tonight or Never* (Mervyn LeRoy, 1931) were a flop, the causes and effects of which were hotly debated in the fashion world — the material of which bankruptcies are made.

---

* The term 'brat pack' refers to a number of American pop stars on the literary scene — Jay McInerney (*Bright Lights, Big City*), Bret Easton Ellis (*Less than Zero*) and Tama Janowitz (*Slaves of New York*).

What had happened? Coco Chanel had not reckoned with the fact that a long time would elapse between the design phase and the film's release. During that time a new and more accentuated silhouette had become fashionable, with longer skirts. Madame Chanel had clung too inflexibly to her models from the late twenties.

In contrast, Givenchy's designs never seem out of date; they retain a timeless elegance. And here we should mention Pierre Balmain too. He served as the costume designer of 73 films (including those of France and England), creating marvelous costumes that brought him great prestige.

When cooperating with full-time Hollywood costume designers, the French far surpassed the American professionals. The work of the famous Edith Head, for instance, for *Sabrina* and *Funny Face* was a gray goose beside a swan next to outfits of Givenchy that were created for these same films. Edith Head willingly admitted that the Oscar for *Sabrina* (1954) should have been shared.

The great French couture houses were also occasionally allowed major roles. As a publicity stunt and in an attempt to give their stars an international aura, the Hollywood studios sometimes sent them to Paris on shopping trips. That photographers happened to go along was part of the project of building a reputation. In the thirties Pola Negri, Mary Pickford, and Louise Brooks asked couturiers with big names and good will to design for them. The bills, running into five and six figures, were of no concern to the stars — big-spending producers charged it all to the advertising accounts (and their calculations paid off). On a visit to Paris in 1925 Gloria Swanson spent a quarter of a million dollars on clothes and furs, most of which were ordered from Patou, at the time the number one haute couture address. The studios took advantage of the cachet of these Paris fashions, spotlighting them in the script. They also made films about the fashion world (one example being *Funny Face*).

For studio costume designers on a fixed salary, there was no such possibility of regarding their creations as independent works of art, then to be integrated into the overall context of the film. Nor did staff designers have any say in what films they would work on; Edith Head, the greatest of them and an eight-time Oscar winner, made this very clear. She has left us a fairly exact description of her scrupulous working methods, and it provides a good picture of how closely the work of the costume designer was interwoven with other aspects of production.

The costume designer is involved right from the start in the preparations for the film, even if only one treatment is possible. The budget has to be very carefully fixed. I start on the designs when the script is ready. Only then can I draw up a dress plot, a score which shows what figure will appear in which scene, at what time of the year, how often and with whom. The most important thing at this stage is to master the script. It prescribes very exactly what one has to design. It contains data on weather conditions, the social and financial status of the individual characters, their personalities, and so on. These studies are the basis for conversations with the director, the producer, and the cast. I always talk to the cast first, ask them how they see their part and how the character should in their view be dressed. Then I speak to the art director, to make sure I do not design a lilac dressing gown for a lilac bedroom; similarly, I talk both to the set and the lighting designers. The effect of a costume very largely depends on their work.

So I do not design the costumes all by myself, I work in close cooperation with all concerned. I do not design *for* people, but *with* people, I believe that is why I have lasted all these years.

Edith Head certainly did last: she continued as head designer for Universal when the other studios had long dropped that title and moved on to other ways of working. From the 1960s they began buying costumes in the boutiques of designers who were now producing ready-to-wear fashion.

Even Audrey Hepburn, who until then had only permitted haute couture, took on ready-to-wear in Stanley Donen's 1966 *Two for the Road*, wearing clothes by Paco Rabanne, Mary Quant, Ken Scott, Michèle Rossier, and others.

From then on Yves Saint Laurent, Gianni Versace, and other couturiers determined the image on the screen, and the influence of the movies on fashion was limited to short-lived looks.

The age of the glamor star was over. The idols were derived from the music and pop scene, and later from television. Julie Harris, who had designed the costumes for *Help!* and *Darling,* among others, complained in 1988 that because fashion had come to mean only 'do whatever you like,' costumes were being less and less frequently custom-designed for the movies. She describes the contemporary procedure as one of simply going to a few of the best-known shops and showing the producer the results of this foray. If the reaction is not favorable, the things are simply exchanged. She points out the similarity between this situation and that of television, a qualified comparison since one episode in a soap opera needs as many changes of costume as a whole feature film.

This trend is evident in the Oscar statistics. In the twenty years following the 1966 prizewinner, *Who's Afraid of Virginia Woolf?,* the award was given only for period rather than contemporary costumes. The only exceptions were *Star Wars* in 1977 and *All That Jazz* in 1979.

Angelika Berg and Regine Engelmeier

Major Costume Designers in Hollywood

ADRIAN (1903–1960), real name Adolph Green-burg, was MGM's leading costume designer from 1928 to 1942. Natasha Rambove, herself a talented designer and married to Rudolph Valentino, discovered Adrian in the twenties and engaged him to design costumes for Valentino. In keeping with the MGM motto 'Do it big, do it right, do it with class,' Adrian designed for films such as Edmund Goulding's 1932 *Grand Hotel* and George Cukor's *Dinner at Eight,* 1933, and his *Women,* 1939. His favorite stars were Greta Garbo, Joan Crawford, and Jean Harlow. He left MGM when Garbo left, opening his own establishment. In 1952 he returned to design for Mervyn LeRoy's *Lovely to Look at,* which included a fashion show of his creations.

TRAVIS BANTON (1894–1958) was made famous by the wedding dress he designed for the 'secret' marriage between Mary Pickford and Douglas Fairbanks. One of his first films for Paramount was *The Dressmaker from Paris* (Paul Bern, 1925), and he designed for a number of historical films, including *The Scarlet Empress* (Josef von Sternberg, 1934) with Marlene Dietrich. His costumes for her were sensational, and his authority so great as to enable him to put her on a diet. However, he had to leave the studio in 1938 owing to heavy drinking. Later he worked at the fashion house of Howard Greer.

CECIL BEATON (1904–1980) was not only a costume designer but also art director and photographer, author, illustrator, designer of stage sets, and many other things. In his function as costume designer he was best known for his work on *Gigi* (Vincente Minnelli, 1958) and *My Fair Lady* (George Cukor, 1964). The latter won him an Oscar. Moviegoers will always remember his costumes for the production of *Anna Karenina* that featured Vivien Leigh (Julien Duvivier, 1948) and for *On a Clear Day You Can See Forever* with Barbra Streisand (Vincente Minnelli, 1970).

HOWARD GREER (1886–1974) was the first costume designer to build up his own department in a studio. He directed the extensive costume department at Paramount, employing 200 tailors and seamstresses. In 1927 he opened his own fashion house, and Travis Banton took over for him at Paramount.

EDITH HEAD (1907–1981) took over the costume department at Paramount when Banton had to leave. She had been assistant to Greer and to Banton. Her intelligence, specialized knowledge, and fairness made her an institution. From 1938 to 1967 she was under contract to Paramount and from then until her death in 1981 to Universal. She won eight Oscars for her design work. She made Barbara Stanwyck a fashion star in *The Lady Eve* (Preston Sturges, 1941) and prior to that, under Banton, clothed the previously unknown Dorothy Lamour in *The Jungle Princess* (William Thiele, 1936). Dorothy Lamour's sarong sparked

Travis Banton and Marlene Dietrich, 1937

Edith Head and Mamie van Doren with costume designs for *Teacher's Pet*, 1958

René Hubert and Marlene Dietrich, 1941

off a fashion craze for tropical materials and motifs. Many actresses insisted on working with Edith Head. Ingrid Bergman asked her to design the costumes for *Notorious* (Alfred Hitchcock, 1946), and Gloria Swanson worked well with her in *Sunset Boulevard* (Billy Wilder, 1950). She was disappointed when Helen Rose was asked to design the wedding dress for her favorite star, Grace Kelly.

RENÉ HUBERT (born in 1899) worked in Berlin, France, England, and Hollywood for both the stage and cinema. His work for *Desirée* (Henry Koster, 1954) and *The Visit* (Bernhard Wicki, 1964) was nominated for Oscars.

IRENE (LENTZ) (1901–1962) worked for seven years from 1942 as chief costume designer for MGM. During that time she designed the costumes for 56 films, including *BF's Daughter* (Robert Z. Leonhard, 1948) and *Midnight Lace* (David Miller, 1960), which was nominated for an Oscar. When her contract with MGM ended, she opened her own fashion house. She was the first leading costume designer to have boutiques inside department stores throughout America.

ROBERT KALLOCH (1893–1943) was of Scottish-American descent. He believed that American

women were better dressed than their European counterparts, who slavishly followed fashion while women in America adapted current trends to their own personalities. In his youth Kalloch designed ballet dresses for Anna Pavlova and worked with the famous fashion designer Lady Duff Gordon (Lucille) in London. He joined Columbia Pictures in Hollywood at the beginning of the thirties. He was a shy, timorous man, afraid of everything and never satisfied with his designs, but he had a sure sense of style and made fantastic sketches. Edith Head said of him: 'Banton is pure fashion, Kalloch pure imagination.'

JEAN LOUIS (born in 1907) began to work for Columbia in 1944. His 'Put the Blame on Mame' dress for Rita Hayworth in *Gilda* (Charles Vidor, 1946) made him famous (see no. 184). He also created particularly beautiful costumes for Marlene Dietrich in *The Monte Carlo Story* (Samuel A. Taylor, 1957).

WALTER ORRY-KELLY (1897–1964) went to Hollywood in 1932 from Australia and worked first for Warner Brothers on the big Busby Berkeley musicals and most of the Bette Davis films. His first major production was *The Rich Are Always with Us* (Alfred E. Green, 1932), and he became widely known for the film *Fashions of 1934* (William

Jean Louis, 1949

Dolores Gray, Helen Rose, and
Lauren Bacall with costume designs
for *Designing Woman*, 1957

William Travilla with Marilyn
Monroe during a fitting for
Gentlemen Prefer Blondes, 1953

Dieterle, 1934), which made Bette Davis a star. In 1943 he became a freelance costume designer, working on productions for Fox, Universal, RKO, and MGM. Orry-Kelly was awarded Oscars for his designs in *An American in Paris* (Vincente Minnelli, 1951) and in *Some Like It Hot* (Billy Wilder, 1959). Other well-known films for which he designed are *Jezebel* (William Wyler, 1938) with Bette Davis, and *Casablanca* (Michael Curtiz, 1942). Orry-Kelly died of cancer in 1964, but it was said in Hollywood that the real cause of his death was a major disappointment. The commission to design *My Fair Lady* (George Cukor, 1964) went not to him but to Cecil Beaton.

WALTER PLUNKETT (1902–1982) began his career with RKO (1926–1939) and then went to MGM (1947–1965), where he experienced a meteoric rise. Historical films were his speciality; his best-known work was *Gone with the Wind* (Victor Fleming, 1939), in which he exactly followed the descriptions of author Margaret Mitchell. No dress was copied more often than that worn by Scarlett O'Hara at the barbecue.

HELEN ROSE (c. 1908) is, with Edith Head and Irene, one of the few women who succeeded in becoming head costume designer at a major studio. After Adrian left she was given that post at

MGM and remained there until 1966, designing for more than two hundred films. Two of them, *The Bad and the Beautiful* (Vincente Minnelli, 1952) and *I'll Cry Tomorrow* (Daniel Mann, 1955) won her Oscars for costume design; altogether she was nominated for eight. Even before leaving the film business, Helen Rose opened her own fashion house; Elizabeth Taylor and Grace Kelly were both married in wedding gowns designed for them by her.

IRENE SHARAFF (c. 1910) came from Broadway to Hollywood to design the costumes for *Meet Me in Saint Louis* (Vincente Minnelli, 1944); she remained to work on a number of musicals. These included *An American in Paris* (Vincente Minnelli, 1951), *West Side Story* (Robert Wise, Jerome Robbins, 1961), and *Funny Girl* (William Wyler, 1968). Sharaff's extravagant designs for Elizabeth Taylor in *Cleopatra* (Joseph L. Mankiewicz, 1953) and in *The Taming of the Shrew* (Franco Zeffirelli, 1967) aroused much attention.

WILLIAM TRAVILLA began at Columbia, was with Warner Brothers for many years, and from 1949 worked for Fox. He was nominated for an Oscar four times. He had good relations with Marilyn Monroe, as was evident in *Gentlemen Prefer Blondes* (Howard Hawks, 1953).

Ponkie

Clothes Make the Man...

... Especially in Hollywood

If film is the subconscious of time, then fashion in film is the clothing of the subconscious. The soul wears petticoats, is the Sphinx, is homespun. We see this chronicled in the classic film *The Time Machine,* when the window display of a London fashion store from the turn of the century to the Second World War is flashed through in time exposure: people as the clothes pegs of their age.

Yet there are problems with this image of synchroneity. One of the things I longed for most when I was a teenager was Marlene Dietrich's casual but sophisticated pantsuit of the early thirties, in which she was photographed on board ship for America, cigarette hanging loosely from the corner of her mouth, hands caught elegantly in the pockets of her trousers (the ultimate in cool!). But her anticipation of feminine fashions in trousers (chic, comfortable, and with no regard for convention: the lady as single, only needing to please herself) did not become generally accepted until thirty years later. Wearing men's slacks remained the preserve of the eccentric international star — a whim of the cinema vamp. And even when women did begin to wear pants, it was quite a long time before the old patriarchs could stop grimacing at female colleagues in them.

So it is not quite true to say that what the movies show becomes fashion, although it might at first appear this way, considering the power of the desire to imitate (every salesclerk a Marilyn Monroe, every schoolgirl a Brigitte Bardot!). A fashion for which the time (or the image of woman) is not yet ripe cannot be established even by a film star. Fashion is the spirit of the time and of life. *It has to be in the air.*

But then there is also the function of the movies as 'dream factory.' This has really changed only in the last twenty years. Films in the thirties, forties, and fifties did not portray reality. They were the purveyors of daydreams. Their milieu was the salon with the white telephone, the millionaire's villa, the luxury hotel, the foyer filled with people in evening dress and tails, the cream of high society in a night bar in Monte Carlo.

If an ordinary woman appeared in these films, poor but pure in body and soul, it was only to play Cinderella and win the boss's son or the count in disguise. He thereupon piled into her wardrobe those clouds of tulle, oceans of silver lamé, white fox capes, and hats with veils that the little dream doll needed as a working dress, so to speak, to be happy ever after.

The ordinary woman did not have the Rockefeller wardrobe, but the Rockefeller world had its feminine types — Doris Day, Jane Russell, Audrey Hepburn. We knew very well how high the eyebrows had to go for the model in question (to be a funny little mouse, a cuddly lamb, or a shy deer, and whether the bosom was to be worn hitched up like Gina Lollobrigida or flat like the fragile teenaged Twiggy. We learned it all at the movies.

The developments were often breathtaking: Romy Schneider shot from the dirndl to the hell-

Liv Ullman in
Autumn Sonata, 1977

fire look, Jane Fonda from *Barbarella* to hippy freedom and back again, while others spanned the entire spectrum of esteem from great lady to mate to mother to prostitute — there was a lot going on.

All the models of fashion in the movies — whether lady, dumb blonde, sexy Lolita, or Meryl Streep in a raincoat, influenced the human eye. What does it think is beautiful? And how long will it see things that way?

If someone turns up in an old cardigan, like Liv Ullman, fashion is besmirched, of course. But that should not detract from our pleasure in the huge range of fashion in films represented in the present volume. A cardigan doesn't count. For people are what they wear — particularly in Hollywood.

The Contributors

REGINE ENGELMEIER, journalist, studied education and history. Conceived of the exhibition *Film und Mode — Mode im Film* and worked on two other exhibitions: *Werkfotos — Hinter den Kulissen des Films* and *Beauty — Star-Gesichter;* responsible for initial selection for the exhibition *Kunst der Standfotografie* in the Museum Ludwig, Cologne.

PETER W. ENGELMEIER, film journalist, studied art history and philosophy. Author of several books, contributor to numerous periodicals, head of two publishing services — Film Manuskripte and Deutscher Fernsehdienst. Owns the largest private collection of film stills in Europe: 1.1 million photographs.

PONKIE, real name Ilse Kümpfel-Schliekmann, is Germany's best-known film critic (writing for the Munich *Abendzeitung*); she has established her reputation through the publication of numerous articles related to cinema.

ANGELIKA BERG, journalist, studied art history. Munich film writer, critic, and contributor to magazines throughout the German-speaking world. Works as an editor for Film Manuskripte.

AUDREY HEPBURN, actress, winner of an Oscar. Ambassador for the United Nations Children's Fund (UNICEF).

MELANIE HILLMER, journalist, studied graphic design and music. Works with a number of magazines, mostly publications that deal with fashion within a sociocultural context.

Further information on the costume design profession and the work of the Verband der Szenenbildner, Filmarchitekten und Kostümbildner (German Association of Stage Designers, Film Architects and Costume Designers) can be obtained from:
SFK Verband e.V., Bavariafilmplatz 7, 82031 Grünwald, Telephone: (089) 6493139.

From the Collection

Seven Decades of Fashion

Our foray through the years: as we leaf through these photographs, people from the twenties to the nineties pass before us, people who lived their lives in films and gave their audiences ideas, inspiration, and hope. Ideas about the spirit of their time. Inspiration for a personal approach to fashion. And hope: hope that their lives could rise to the level of the stars by clothing themselves in the same fashion.

Although it is conceivable, a svelte black evening dress alone does not make a Dorothy Lamour, a supercool glance full of distant longing does not make a Pola Negri, nor does a petticoat and bustier with a bare midriff make a Madonna. The leather jacket is not what makes Kelly McGillis, nor the red dress Kelly LeBrock. But it's fun to copy the outfits on our real-life level, and no one need feel victimized by fashion.

1 Pola Negri, 1924

2   Katherine Griffith, Mary Pickford in *Pollyanna*, 1920

3   Cullen Landis, Helene Costello in *The Lights of New York*, 1928

4
Janet Gaynor,
Charles Farrell
in *Sunny Side Up*,
1929

5
Gloria Swanson
in the twenties

6   Mervyn LeRoy, Colleen Moore in the twenties

7   Madge Bellamy, Leslie Fenton in *Black Paradise*, 1926

8   Mae Murray in *The Merry Widow*, 1925

9
Jeanette
MacDonald
in *Magic Ring*,
1929

10
Greta Garbo,
Nils Asther in
The Single Standard,
1929

11
Conrad Nagel,
Greta Garbo in
The Mysterious Lady,
1928

12
Greta Garbo,
Jacques Feyder in
Anna Christie,
1929

13   Rita Cansino (Rita Hayworth), Astrid Allwyn in *Dante's Inferno*, 1935

14   Gary Cooper, Claudette Colbert, Ernst Lubitsch on the set
of *Bluebeard's Eighth Wife*, 1938

15 Greta Garbo, Melvyn Douglas in *Ninotchka*, 1939

16   Peggy Fears in
Lottery Lover, 1935

17   Clark Gable, Norma Shearer in *Idiot's Delight*, 1939

18
Clark Gable,
Claudette Colbert in
It Happened One Night,
1934

19 Lilian Harvey, 1934

20 Myrna Loy in *The Mask of Fu Manchu*, 1932

21
Accessories for
The Divorce of Lady X,
1938

22
Laura Hope Crews,
Marlene Dietrich
in *Angel*,
1937

23   Marlene Dietrich, John Halliday in *Desire*, 1936

24 Marlene Dietrich, 1934

25   Eve Arden, Jinx Falkenburg, Otto Kruger, Anita Colby in *Cover Girl*, 1944

26   Ann Sothern, Eleanor Powell
in *Lady Be Good*, 1941

27   Hedy Lamarr, 1938

28   Anne Nagel, Constance Moore, 1940

29   Jean Rogers, 1940

30   Judy Garland, 1941

31   Paulette Goddard, 1941

32   Bette Davis in *A Stolen Life*, 1946

33   Lilli Palmer, 1947

34   Rona Anderson in *Floodtide*, 1949

35   Margaret Lockwood in *Bad Sister*, 1947

36 Ginger Rogers in *Lady in the Dark*, 1944

38
Audrey Hepburn
in *Roman Holiday*,
1953

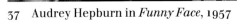

37   Audrey Hepburn in *Funny Face*, 1957

39
Audrey Hepburn
in *Funny Face*,
1957

40   Audrey Hepburn in *Funny Face*, 1957

41   Mitzi Gaynor in *Anything Goes*, 1956

42 Sophia Loren in *Boy on a Dolphin*, 1957

43 Jayne Mansfield in *Will Success Spoil Rock Hunter?*, 1957

44 Joan Collins in *I Believe in You*, 1952

45 Marilyn Monroe, Tom Ewell in *The Seven Year Itch*, 1955

46   Sophia Loren in *La Ciociara*, 1960

47   Anita Ekberg in *Artists and Models*, 1955

48 Jack Palance, Corinne Calvert in
Flight to Tangier, 1953

49 Marilyn Monroe in the fifties

50 Nadja Tiller in *Das Mädchen Rosemarie*, 1958

51 Elke Sommer in *Auf Wiedersehen*, 1960

52   Brigitte Bardot during shooting for *La Vie privée*, 1961

53
Brigitte Bardot
in the sixties

54
Brigitte Bardot
in *Les Novices*,
1970

55   Jacqueline Bisset in *Bullitt*, 1968

56   Raquel Welch in *Roustabout*, 1964

57   Daliah Lavi, Laurence Harvey in *The Spy with A Cold Nose*, 1966

58   Glenna Forster-Jones, Geneviève Waite in *Joanna*, 1968

59 Marcello Mastroianni, Sophia Loren in *La moglie del prete*, 1970

60   Peter Sellers in *I Love You, Alice B. Toklas,* 1968

61 Natalie Wood, Ian Bannen in *Penelope*, 1966

62 Yves Montand, Barbra Streisand
in *On a Clear Day You Can See Forever*, 1970

63
Britt Ekland
in *The Bobo*,
1967

64
Charlotte Rampling
in *La Chair de l'Orchidée*,
1974

65
Elke Sommer
in the seventies

66 Ali MacGraw in *Love Story*, 1970

67 Jodie Foster in *Taxi Driver*, 1976

68 Audrey Hepburn in *Bloodline*, 1979

69 Barbra Streisand in *A Star Is Born*, 1976

70   Madonna in *Who's That Girl?*, 1987

71   Melanie Griffith in *Something Wild*, 1987

72   Chloe Webb, Gary Oldman in *Sid and Nancy*, 1986

73
Bernadette Peters,
Mercedes Ruehl in
Slaves of New York,
1989

74   Isabelle Adjani in *Mortelle Randonnée*, 1983

75   Diane Keaton in *Baby Boom*, 1987

76   Kelly McGillis in *Top Gun*, 1986

77   Cher, 1986

78   The Gaultier Look: Helen Mirren in *The Cook, the Thief, His Wife and Her Lover*, 1989

Heading for the Year 2000 with YY

For the fashion world the trend as we approach the millennium is: *the naughty nineties.* With Peter Greenaway's unappetizing orgy *The Cook, the Thief, His Wife and Her Lover,* the decade cast its shadow in Jean-Paul Gaultier's red and black, as a fashion-maker tried to propagate himself as a cinematic costume designer. However, there was little future in it, for his clothes were actually a retrograde reference to the sort of thing we are all too familiar with (see adjacent photograph). As 'masterfully simple but impudent outfits' (*Der Spiegel*) predominate in the early nineties, designers like Giorgio Armani (*The Untouchables*) and Nino Cerruti (who provided the elegance of *Wall Street*) will likely have their say.

Top designers are moving back onto the film track. What they want is publicity and sales. A hero in Bognor, a leading lady in Saint Laurent or Dior-Ferré means prestige for the designer. Meanwhile the guru of fashion, Yohji Yamamoto, is forecasting the continuance of his 'people-friendly' line. The first film of the nineties on the subject of fashion comes from Wim Wenders, both the writer and director of *Aufzeichnungen zu Kleidern und Städten* (*Notes on Clothes and Cities*), which began showing in theaters in April of 1990. This fascinating documentary concerns itself with Yamamoto, whom Wenders experiences as a kindred inventive spirit, a man of his own time and kind. YY certainly provides strong directives for cinematic costume design in the nineties. He was ahead of his time years ago.

R. E.

79
Yohji Yamamoto and his team at work. Scene from *Aufzeichnungen zu Kleidern und Städten*, 1989

Trend-Setting Films

Audrey Hepburn as Holly Golightly peers through dark glasses into the window at Tiffany's (no. 85). With her lavish jewels she is herself a stylized object on display. In her little black Givenchy dress she moves, a perfect fashion model, through *Breakfast at Tiffany's* (Blake Edwards, 1961). Billy Wilder predicted that she would put the bust out of style. In 1989 and 1990 Holly Golightly was back again as a party girl, proof of how ravishingly films can revive fashions. Audrey Hepburn is currently more 'in' than Meryl Streep (whose *Out of Africa* costume was eagerly seized upon by retailers), and all this has followed such phenomena as the Bonnie-and-Clyde midi, or the Gatsby look that swept 1973 and 1974.

Fashion booms through the cinema. And every fashion flows right into film, making the cinema a document of its time. Or time itself may become documentary: the trends of former years may be taken up again by the rag trade, and the stars from the good old days of the movies can enjoy a comeback.

80   Mia Farrow, Robert Redford in *The Great Gatsby*, 1974

81   Claude Rains, Paul Henreid, Humphrey Bogart, Ingrid Bergman in *Casablanca*, 1943

82   James Dean in *Rebel without a Cause*, 1955

83
Jean-Paul Belmondo,
Jean Seberg
in *A bout de souffle*,
1959

84
Brigitte Bardot
in *Et Dieu créa la femme*,
1956

85   Audrey Hepburn in *Breakfast at Tiffany's*, 1960

86   Robert Shaw, Robert Redford, Paul Newman in *The Sting*, 1974

87   Meryl Streep in *Out of Africa*, 1986

88   Faye Dunaway, Warren Beatty in *Bonnie and Clyde*, 1967

89   Antonio Gades, Laura del Sol in *Carmen*, 1983

90   Madonna in *Desperately Seeking Susan*, 1985

Hats

Hedy Lamarr once said that she felt naked without something on her head. Now we know why she appeared on screen with any number of extravagant shapes integrated into her hairdo. The stars liked best to don superhats for photo calls, but they had to bow to the will of the costume designer — no matter how the hat suited their face. Jane Fonda might well have been even more erotic in *Klute* if she had not been forced to wear that black unmentionable on her progressive short haircut (no. 132), while Alec Guinness as an old spinster in *Kind Hearts and Coronets* was helped by the bird he/she had to wear (no. 121).

Most certainly the 'Pancake Look' was inspired by the spring hat that designer Madge Chard dumped on the head of eighteen-year-old Joan Collins for her first leading role, in *I Believe in You* (no. 127). Audrey Hepburn also started a hat boom in 1957 when she enchanted her audiences with her quiet elegance in *Funny Face* (no. 126).

Trend-setter Marlene Dietrich, who adopted a kind of beret to go with her menswear (she wore the same, along with costumes by Dior, selected by Margaret Furse, in *Journey into the Unknown*, 1951), wanted all women to be free of the constraints and conventions of female fashion. It was the self-confident postulate of a great and influential star. We take off our hats to her.

91 The designer Irene working for MGM

92
Gloria Swanson
in the twenties

93
Asta Nielsen
in *Erdgeist*,
1923

94   Jeanette MacDonald in the twenties

95   Greta Garbo in *Mata Hari*, 1931

96   Greta Garbo in *The Painted Veil*, 1934

97
Marlene Dietrich
in *The Lady Is Willing*,
1942

98
Zarah Leander
in *La Habanera*,
1937

99   Hedy Lamarr in *Dishonored Lady*, 1947

100   Dorothy Lovett in *Powder Town*, 1942

101   Ruth Warrick in *Arch of Triumph*, 1948

102   Greer Garson in *Random Harvest*, 1942

103   Myrna Loy, 1940

104　Patricia Morison in *The Roundup*, 1941

105   Martha Vickers, 1946

106   Ann Sothern in *Gold Rush Maisie*, 1940

107   Dorothy Lamour in *My Favorite Brunette*, 1947

108   Joan Crawford, 1940

109   Rita Hayworth in *Tonight and Every Night*, 1944

110   Marlene Dietrich in *No Highway in the Sky*, 1951

111   Lauren Bacall in *The Big Sleep*, 1946

112   Judy Garland in *For Me and My Gal*, 1942

113   Marguerite Chapman in *Mr. District Attorney*, 1946

114   Merle Oberon in *Temptation*, 1946

115   Gloria Swanson, 1941

116   Rosalind Russell in *The Women*, 1939

118
Loretta Young in
The Men in Her Life,
1941

117   Ruth Warrick, 1941

119
Sylvia Sidney in
The Searching Wind,
1946

120   Olivia de Havilland in *Hold Back the Dawn*, 1941

121   Alec Guinness in *Kind Hearts and Coronets*, 1949

122
Dolores del Rio
in *Journey into Fear*,
1942

123
Deborah Kerr
in the fifties

124   Jane Russell in *Son of Paleface*, 1952

125   Jean Seberg in *Bonjour Tristesse*, 1958

126
Audrey Hepburn
in *Funny Face*,
1957

127   Joan Collins in *I Believe in You*, 1952

128
Sophia Loren
in *Arabesque*,
1966

129
Audrey Hepburn in
How to Steal a Million,
1966

130 Shirley MacLaine in *What a Way to Go!*, 1964

131
Ali MacGraw,
1971

132
Jane Fonda
in *Klute*,
1971

133   Brigitte Bardot in *L'Ours et la poupée*, 1970

Hair

There have been few changes in the style of poodle dressing over the years, but filmstars, both male and female, have gone through a range of hairstyles. Seeing the devotion with which Hollywood hairdresser Gertrude Wheeler dresses the voluptuous curls of Joan Crawford while the star combs the head of her poodle is a study in the art of grooming.

Works of art on the heads of ladies, designed and executed by master coiffeurs, are an essential part of the total work of art as many costume designers see it. What could be made of beautiful women with the help of the permanent wave, hairspray and dryer appears in a particularly ravishing way in stills of Loretta Young (no. 141), Rita Hayworth (nos. 142, 144), Lilli Palmer (no. 143), and Brigitte Helm (no. 136; a miracle of blonde waves). In contrast we see the provocative short cuts of Shirley MacLaine (no. 149), Jean Seberg (no. 245), and 'Sabrina' Hepburn (no. 148). This is hair to catch the eye, as a fetish or encore — from Veronica Lake, the Rapunzel of the cinema, to Cher, whose self-designed hairdos compete with her often hair-raising wardrobe.

And then there are the heads of men, from the melting smoothness of the young Yves Montand (no. 150) to Elvis Presley (no. 151), who brought the makers of Brillcream a fortune and who shone at least as brightly as Yul Brynner's bald head (no. 152).

Ali MacGraw (no. 153) certainly deserves special attention, wearing her black Indian-Squaw hair in the purist fashion of the sixties and early seventies, with a center part that was imitated by at least as many women as followed Cher (no. 157) or the punk Isabelle Adjani (no. 154).

134   Joan Crawford with her poodle *Cliquot* and hairstylist Gertrude Wheeler, 1950

135 Myrna Loy, 1936

136   Brigitte Helm in *Fürst Woronzeff*, 1934

137   Merle Oberon in *Temptation*, 1946

138   Virginia Mayo, 1954

139   Eleanor Parker, 1947

140
Paula Corday in
Too Young to Kiss,
1951

141   Loretta Young in *The Men in Her Life*, 1941

142   Rita Hayworth, 1942

143   Lilli Palmer, 1947

144   Rita Hayworth, 1946

145   John Wayne, Marlene Dietrich in *The Spoilers*, 1942

146 Elizabeth Taylor in *Rhapsody*, 1954

147 Hildegard Knef in *Diplomatic Courier*, 1952

148 Audrey Hepburn, 1953

149 Shirley MacLaine, 1960

150
Yves Montand,
1944

151 Elvis Presley, 1960

152
Yul Brynner
in *The Journey*,
1959

153   Ali MacGraw in *Love Story*, 1970

154   Isabelle Adjani in *Subway*, 1985

155   Marisa Berenson in *Barry Lyndon*, 1975

156   Barbara Bach in *The Humanoid*, 1979

157 Cher, 1986

Evening Dresses

The glittering of the evening stars and the film-stars — a symbiosis that is the fabric from which the night is made. Silk, taffeta, velvet seduce. The ladies come downstairs, slide out of cars looking impossibly feminine in rustling lace dresses under fur stoles, spend longer than they really should carefully adjusting the well-slit skirt, fan themselves a little, although the décolleté shows how coolly the lady is enjoying the moment — the great evening dress in film is part of the world of art.

Some of the transparent dreams caused a sensation. They implied that ordinary women, too, might find a man if they wore dresses like these, a man to get the stars down from the sky for them. Mae West had two versions of the same breathtaking evening dress by designer Travis Banton — one to walk and stand in, and one in which she could sit down, the perfect female larva, without bursting out of it.

158   Jane Russell in *The Revolt of Mamie Stover*, 1956

159   Mae West in *Every Day's a Holiday*, 1938

160   Jeanette MacDonald in *The Firefly*, 1937

161   Clark Gable, Norma Shearer in *Idiot's Delight*, 1939

162
Clark Gable,
Jean Harlow
in *Saratoga*,
1937

163   Barbara Stanwyck, 1940

164   Olivia de Havilland in *The Male Animal*, 1942

165   Hedy Lamarr in *Crossroads*, 1942

166   Carole Lombard in *To Be or Not to Be*, 1942

167   Annabella, 1939

168
Marlene Dietrich
in *Seven Sinners*,
1940

169
Marlene Dietrich in
The Devil Is a Woman,
1935

170   Marlene Dietrich in *A Foreign Affair*, 1948

171
Paulette Goddard (second from left),
Joan Crawford (third from left),
Rosalind Russell (fourth from left),
Norma Shearer (second from right),
Mary Boland (on bed)
in *The Women*, 1939

172
Marguerite Chapman in
One Way to Love,
1946

173 Joan Crawford in *Dancing Lady*, 1933

174
Sylvia Sidney
in *Blood on the Sun*,
1945

175   Myrna Loy in *The Rains Came*, 1939

176   Claudette Colbert in *The Palm Beach Story*, 1942

177   Lilli Palmer in *Body and Soul*, 1947

178   Dorothy Lamour, 1939

179   Ginger Rogers in *Magnificent Doll*, 1946

180   Maureen O'Hara in *How Green Was My Valley*, 1941

181   Joan Leslie in *Hollywood Canteen*, 1944

182   Loretta Young in *A Night to Remember*, 1942

183   Rita Hayworth in *Cover Girl*, 1944

184   Rita Hayworth in *Gilda*, 1946

185   Suzy Parker, 1957

186   Anita Ekberg in *Artists and Models*, 1955

187   Shirley MacLaine in *What a Way to Go!*, 1964

188   Elizabeth Taylor in *Elephant Walk*, 1954

189   Elizabeth Taylor in *Julia Misbehaves*, 1948

190   Marilyn Monroe in *All about Eve*, 1950

191   Marilyn Monroe in *The Prince and the Showgirl*, 1957

192   Pier Angeli in *The Flame and the Flesh*, 1954

193   Ann Todd, 1948

194   Grace Kelly, Frank Sinatra in *High Society*, 1956

195   Grace Kelly in *Dial M for Murder*, 1954

196 Ava Gardner at the premiere of *The Barefoot Contessa*, 1954

197   Audrey Hepburn in *Funny Face*, 1957

198   Patricia Morison in *The Roundup*, 1941

199
Jayne Mansfield,
Tom Ewell in
The Girl Can't Help It,
1956

200   Betty Grable in *How to Marry a Millionaire*, 1953

201   Sabrina at Ascot, 1957

202   Elsa Martinelli, 1956

203 Deborah Kerr in *The King and I*, 1956

204 Audrey Hepburn in *Sabrina*, 1954

205
Tina Louise,
1959

206 Sophia Loren, 1958

Gloves

The signals of sensuality are transmitted all the more intensely through the veiled sender. Disrobing increases the tension — there can be no doubt of that.

The glove, rolled up or dropped on the floor deliberately but as if by accident to mark the start of a feud, stripped off with passion or pulled slowly and seductively from the tips of the fingers in an arm and finger striptease, is one of the special signals that designers of all periods have used again and again (we need only think of Thiery Mugler, Jean-Paul Gaultier, and Yohji Yamamoto). Gloves are still eagerly sought-after accessories.

In silk or suede, plastic or gold lamé, the glove has had its hand in the game for many stars. Rita Hayworth's entrance in *Gilda* was unforgettable, and so was Marlene with gloves cut to reveal her fingertips, enabling her to grasp the cigarette that was smoked so sensuously. Greta Garbo's regal handling of the gloves in *Anna Karenina,* Grace Kelly's combination of dress, scarf, and gloves, and Susanna Foster's and Irene Dunne's net fantasies provide more images of this fashionable and dramatic ten-finger system that has so many functions to fulfill.

207   Gene Tierney, 1942

208   Susanna Foster, 1945

209   Irene Dunne in *Sweet Adeline*, 1955

210
Dorothy Shay
in *Comin' Round
the Mountain*, 1951

211   Vera Ellen, 1952

212
Carmen Miranda in
Something for the Boys,
1944

213
Grace Kelly in
To Catch a Thief,
1955

214 Grace Kelly in *Rear Window*, 1954

Men's Fashions

Casual relaxation or the great school of the beau, English tweed of salt and pepper, the elegant tails, the mustached hero who copes with the most difficult situations, and the hatted gentlemen of the twilight variety — all these had their imitators among their public, fans who wanted the pinstripe culture or the romance of the lumberjack in their own private lives. Tailor-made suits set sartorial standards. If Clark Gable dried a lady's tears with the pocket handkerchief that was always at hand, the ladies in their seats cried gently as well, and their companions hastened to appear at the next trip to the movies with a handkerchief at hand in their breast pockets too …

The rebels of yesteryear in their T-shirts and leather jackets, granddads of the Punks, fascinated millions of real fans, and the no-iron costume design era squealed under the wheels of James Dean's Porsche.

Then Mad Max took up the trail, and today the relatively smart types from the Brando era are back. The man of today lives again East of Eden.

215 David Niven, 1935

216
Charles Ray in
The Girl I Loved,
1923

217
Errol Flynn
in *The Charge of
the Light Brigade,*
1936

218   Henry Fonda in *I Met My Love Again*, 1938

219 Alec Guinness in *Kind Hearts and Coronets*, 1949

220   Lewis Stone in the thirties

221   George Gobel, David Niven during
the filming of *The Birds and the Bees*, 1956

222   Walter Connolly, Guy Kibbee in
Lady for a Day, 1933

223   Michael Trubshaw, David Niven
during a break in shooting, 1952

224　Yves Montand, 1961

225　Walter Pidgeon, 1943

226　Jean Gabin in *La Bête humaine*, 1938

227　Daniel Day Lewis in *A Room with a View*, 1986

228   Jean Louis in the forties

229   Tyrone Power, 1942

230   Clark Gable in *Any Number Can Play*, 1949

231   Humphrey Bogart, 1939

232   Dirk Bogarde, 1950

233   Ronald Reagan, 1947

234   Cary Grant, John Williams in *To Catch a Thief*, 1955

235   Marlon Brando in *A Streetcar Named Desire*, 1951

236   Anthony Perkins in *The Actress*, 1953

237   John Wayne, 1953

238   Paul Newman in *Somebody Up There Likes Me*, 1956

239 Burt Lancaster in *The Kentuckian*, 1955

240 Richard Widmark in *The Law and Jake Wade*, 1958

241 Ernest Borgnine in *The Catered Affair*, 1956

242 Elvis Presley in *Flaming Star*, 1960

243
Marlon Brando,
Fred Zinnemann,
Montgomery Clift
on the set for
The Young Lions,
1958

244
James Dean,
Corey Allen in
*Rebel without
a Cause*, 1955

245   Jean-Paul Belmondo, Jean Seberg in *A bout de souffle*, 1959

246   Horst Buchholz in *Das Totenschiff*, 1959

247   Marlon Brando in *A Streetcar Named Desire*, 1951

248
Marcello Mastroianni
in *La dolce vita*,
1961

249   Peter Fonda (right) in *Easy Rider*, 1969

250   *The Wanderers*, 1979 (the film is set in the sixties)

251   Julie Christie, Warren Beatty in *Shampoo*, 1975

252   Donald Sutherland in *Steelyard Blues*, 1973

253   *Mad Max 2 — The Road Warrior*, 1982

254   Kevin Costner in *The Untouchables*, 1987

255   Jack Nicholson in *The Witches of Eastwick*, 1987

256
Arsenio Hall,
Eddie Murphy
in *Coming to
America*, 1988

Period Costumes

Where reliable sources in history exist and can be used, the task of the costume designers is presumably easier. They adapt and occasionally add a dash of 'taste' cautiously and subtly, and with practical considerations in mind, for the cut of clothes that are historically accurate rarely suits the demands of an action film.

Is there little scope for imagination and creativity? On the contrary. The ladies and gentlemen brought up from the dark depths of history have period costumes produced for them in which the designer has had a strong hand, while the clothes worn by fictitious figures from not clearly defined periods have always afforded scope for fashionable invention, especially in the great Hollywood studios.

To combine delicacy, exactness of detail, and the authenticity that in turn makes the whole work believable — that was the formula for the period costumes in films like *Marie Antoinette* (costumes by Adrian, Gile Steele) or *Gone with the Wind* (costumes by Walter Plunkett).

Historical costuming is the perfect combination of the arts of the designer and the tailor. This volume contains mainly examples from films made before 1948, and many of them were worthy of an Oscar. However, an Oscar for Costume Design, that eagerly sought-after award, was only given after 1948 (a list of these is included on page 192).

257   Hedy Lamarr in *Lady of the Tropics*, 1939

258   Greta Garbo in *Camille*, 1936

259
Greta Garbo
in *Queen Christina*,
1933

260
Greta Garbo,
Ramon Novarro
in *Mata Hari*,
1931

261   Greta Garbo in *Conquest*, 1937

262   Greta Garbo, Fredric March in *Anna Karenina*, 1935

263   Robert Taylor, Greta Garbo in *Camille*, 1936

264   Marlene Dietrich in *Kismet*, 1944

265   Marlene Dietrich in *Golden Earrings*, 1947

Catherine
the Great

266   Marlene Dietrich as Catherine the Great in *The Scarlet Empress*, 1934

267
Marlene Dietrich
in *The Scarlet
Empress*, 1934

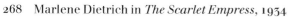

268   Marlene Dietrich in *The Scarlet Empress*, 1934

269   Marlene Dietrich in *The Scarlet Empress*, 1934

270
Pola Negri as
Catherine the Great,
Rod La Rocque in
Forbidden Paradise,
1924

271
Joan Gardner,
Douglas Fairbanks Jr.
in *Catherine the Great*,
1934

272   Brigitte Horney as Catherine the Great in *Münchhausen*, 1942

273
Tallulah
Bankhead as
Catherine
the Great
in *A Royal
Scandal*, 1945

274
Peter O'Toole,
Jeanne Moreau
in *Great
Catherine*, 1968

Contemporary
portrait of
Cleopatra
on a coin

275   Theda Bara in *Cleopatra*, 1917

276
Claudette
Colbert
in *Cleopatra*,
1934

277   Rhonda Fleming as Cleopatra in
Serpent of the Nile, 1953

278   Elizabeth Taylor, Rex Harrison in *Cleopatra*, 1963

279   Vivien Leigh, Flora Robson in *Caesar and Cleopatra*, 1946

Queen
Victoria

280   Gaby Morlay as Queen Victoria in *Entente cordiale*, 1939

281   Irene Dunne as Queen Victoria in
The Mudlark, 1950

282   Anton Walbrook (Adolf Wohlbrück),
Anna Neagle in *Victoria the Great*, 1937

283
Anton Walbrook,
Anna Neagle in
Victoria the Great,
1937

284   Gabriel Gabrio, Edwige Feuillère in *Lucrezia Borgia*, 1937

285   Dick Powell, Olivia de Havilland in *A Midsummer Night's Dream*, 1935

286
Gladys George,
Joseph Schild-
kraut in *Marie
Antoinette*, 1938

287   Scene from *Marie Antoinette*, 1938

288
Scene from
Münchhausen,
1942

289
Hans Albers,
Hubert von Meyerinck
in *Münchhausen*,
1942

290
Mona Maris

291
Alice Faye in
In Old Chicago,
1938

292   Merle Oberon in *A Night in Paradise*, 1946

293   Clark Gable, Vivien Leigh in *Gone with the Wind*, 1939

294   Ingrid Bergman in *Saratoga Trunk*, 1945

An Oscar for Costume Design

A naked figure as an award for specialists to whom nothing on earth is more important than dressing their fellow men: the Oscar for Costume Design, awarded only since 1948, honors tailors and designers for a wealth of invention that is effective only within the overall context of a film's production. The list of winners is not very long: the names of Edith Head and Irene Sharaff appear again and again when the statuettes are retrieved from the treasury of the dream factory. In 1987 and 1988 the award was won by a man whom the film world unstintingly acknowledged as 'King of Costume' (*Variety*): James Acheson gave us the opulent wardrobes of Bernardo Bertolucci's *The Last Emperor* and Stephen Frears's *Dangerous Liaisons* (which started another décolleté comeback).

The Oscar is indisputably the ultimate nonfinancial reward, and the winner can be sure of a crossfire of criticism and attack from his or her colleagues. In the fashion world remarks on the decisions of the jury, ranging from sharp to ugly, have become tradition.

Particularly, there were protests from many quarters and countries at what seemed arbitrary choices when the Award for Costume Design was given for the films *West Side Story* by Robert Wise and Jerome Robbins, *Chariots of Fire* by Hugh Hudson, *Gandhi* by Richard Attenborough, and *Amadeus* by Miloš Forman. But unanimous approval has been known as well. When *Barry Lyndon*, Stanley Kubrick's pastel dream story, won the costume Oscar (designers Ulla-Britt Søderlund and Milena Canonero), the film world had been expecting the decision, and in this case the golden trophy was virtually steered in the right direction with the help of benevolent American ad-men.

The Academy of Motion Picture Arts and Sciences of the United States has given an Oscar every year since 1948 for Costume Design. The following is a list of all the winners of the award. Until 1966 a distinction was drawn between black and white (b/w) and color (c) films. The date is the year the award was given.

Year		Title	Award winner(s)
1948	b/w	*Hamlet*	Roger K. Furse
	c	*Joan of Arc*	Dorothy Jeakins, Karinska
1949	b/w	*The Heiress*	Edith Head, Gile Steele
	c	*The Adventures of Don Juan*	Leah Rhodes, William Travilla, Marjorie Best
1950	b/w	*All about Eve*	Edith Head, Charles LeMaire
	c	*Samson and Delilah*	Edith Head, Dorothy Jeakins, Elois Jenssen, Gile Steele, Gwen Wakeling
1951	b/w	*A Place in the Sun*	Edith Head
	c	*An American in Paris*	Orry-Kelly, Walter Plunkett, Irene Sharaff
1952	b/w	*The Bad and the Beautiful*	Helen Rose
	c	*Moulin Rouge*	Marcel Vertes
1953	b/w	*Roman Holiday*	Edith Head
	c	*The Robe*	Charles LeMaire, Emile Santiago
1954	b/w	*Sabrina*	Edith Head
	c	*Jigokumon*	Sanzo Wada
1955	b/w	*I'll Cry Tomorrow*	Helen Rose
	c	*Love Is a Many-Splendored Thing*	Charles LeMaire

295 Costume designer Edith Head with her eight Oscars

Year		Title	Award winner(s)
1956	b/w	*The Solid Gold Cadillac*	Jean Louis
	c	*The King and I*	Irene Sharaff
1957	b/w	*Les Girls*	Orry-Kelly
1958	c	*Gigi*	Cecil Beaton
1959	b/w	*Some Like It Hot*	Orry-Kelly
	c	*Ben Hur*	Elizabeth Haffenden
1960	b/w	*The Facts of Life*	Edith Head, Edward Stevenson
	c	*Spartacus*	Valles, Bill Thomas
1961	b/w	*La dolce vita*	Piero Gherardi
	c	*West Side Story*	Irene Sharaff
1962	b/w	*Whatever Happened to Baby Jane*	Norma Koch
	c	*The Wonderful World of the Brothers Grimm*	Mary Wills
1963	b/w	*Otto e mezzo*	Piero Gherardi
	c	*Cleopatra*	Irene Sharaff, Vittorio Nino Novarese
1964	b/w	*The Night of the Iguana*	Dorothy Jeakins
	c	*My Fair Lady*	Cecil Beaton
1965	b/w	*Darling*	Julie Harris
	c	*Doctor Zhivago*	Phyllis Dalton
1966	b/w	*Who's Afraid of Virginia Woolf*	Irene Sharaff
	c	*A Man for All Seasons*	Elizabeth Haffenden, Joan Bridge
1967		*Camelot*	John Truscott
1968		*Giuletta e Romeo*	Danilo Donati
1969		*Anne of the Thousand Days*	Margaret Furse
1970		*Cromwell*	Vittorio Nino Novarese
1971		*Nicholas and Alexandra*	Yvonne Blake, Antonio Castillo
1972		*Travels with My Aunt*	Anthony Powell
1973		*The Sting*	Edith Head
1974		*The Great Gatsby*	Theoni V. Aldredge
1975		*Barry Lyndon*	Ulla-Britt Søderlund, Milena Canonero
1976		*Il Casanova di Fellini*	Danilo Donati
1977		*Star Wars*	John Mollo
1978		*Death on the Nile*	Anthony Powell
1979		*All That Jazz*	Albert Wolsky
1980		*Tess*	Anthony Powell
1981		*Chariots of Fire*	Milena Canonero
1982		*Gandhi*	John Mollo, Bhanu Athaiya
1983		*Fanny och Alexander*	Marik Vos
1984		*Amadeus*	Theodor Pistek
1985		*Ran*	Emi Wada
1986		*A Room with a View*	Jenny Beavan, John Bright
1987		*The Last Emperor*	James Acheson
1988		*Dangerous Liaisons*	James Acheson
1989		*Henry V*	Phyllis Dalton
1990		*Cyrano de Bergérac*	Franca Squarciapino
1991		*Bugsy*	Albert Wolsky
1992		*Bram Stoker's Dracula*	Eiko Ishioka
1993		*The Age of Innocence*	Gabriella Pescucci
1994		*The Adventures of Priscilla, Queen of Desert*	Lizzy Gardiner
1995		*Restoration*	James Acheson

296
Ingrid Bergman,
José Ferrer
in *Joan of Arc*,
1948

297   Jean Simmons, Laurence Olivier in *Hamlet*, 1948

298   Montgomery Clift, Olivia de Havilland
in *The Heiress*, 1949

299   Errol Flynn, Viveca Lindfors in *The Adventures of Don Juan*, 1949

300   Anne Baxter, Bette Davis, Marilyn Monroe, George Sanders in *All about Eve*, 1950

301   Victor Mature, Hedy Lamarr in *Samson and Delilah*, 1950

302   Elizabeth Taylor, Montgomery Clift in *A Place in the Sun*, 1951

303   Gene Kelly, Leslie Caron in *An American in Paris*, 1951

304   Lana Turner, Kirk Douglas in *The Bad and the Beautiful*, 1952

305
Zsa Zsa Gabor,
José Ferrer
in *Moulin Rouge*,
1952

306
Gregory Peck,
Eddie Albert,
Audrey Hepburn
in *Roman Holiday*,
1953

307
Jean Simmons,
Richard Burton
in *The Robe*,
1953

308   Humphrey Bogart, Audrey Hepburn, William Holden in *Sabrina*, 1954

309   Machiko Kyo, Kazuo Hasegawa in *Jigokumon*, 1954

310   Susan Hayward in *I'll Cry Tomorrow*, 1955

311   Jennifer Jones in *Love Is a Many —
Splendored Thing*, 1955

312   Yul Brynner, Deborah Kerr in *The King and I*, 1956

313
Paul Douglas,
Judy Holliday
in *The Solid
Gold Cadillac*,
1956

314   Kay Kendall, Mitzi Gaynor, Taina Elg in *Les Girls*, 1957

315   Leslie Caron, Louis Jourdan in *Gigi*, 1958

316   Joe E. Brown, Jack Lemmon in *Some Like It Hot*, 1959

317   Charlton Heston, Haya Harareet in *Ben Hur*, 1959

318   Kirk Douglas in *Spartacus*, 1960

319   Bob Hope, Lucille Ball in *The Facts of Life*, 1960

320   Nadia Gray, Marcello Mastroianni in *La dolce vita*, 1961

321
Natalie Wood,
Richard Beymer
in *West Side Story*,
1961

322   Joan Crawford, Bette Davis in *Whatever Happened to Baby Jane?*, 1962

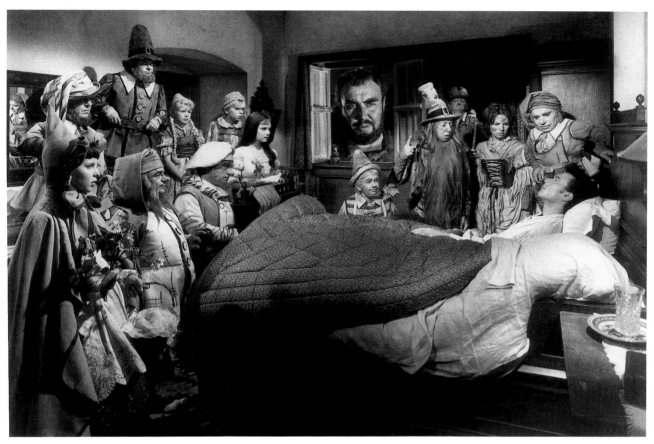

323   Laurence Harvey in *The Wonderful World of the Brothers Grimm*, 1962

324
Claudia Cardinale
in *Otto e mezzo*,
1963

325   Elizabeth Taylor in *Cleopatra*, 1963

326   Sue Lyon, Richard Burton in *The Night of the Iguana*, 1964

327
Audrey Hepburn
in *My Fair Lady*,
1964

328
Laurence Harvey,
Julie Christie,
Dirk Bogarde
in *Darling*,
1965

329
Geraldine Chaplin,
Omar Sharif
in *Doctor Zhivago*,
1965

330
Richard Burton,
Elizabeth Taylor
in *Who's Afraid
of Virginia Woolf?*,
1966

331   Robert Shaw in *A Man for All Seasons*, 1966

332   Richard Harris, Vanessa Redgrave, Franco Nero
in *Camelot*, 1967

333
Leonard Whiting,
Olivia Hussey in
Romeo and Juliet,
1968

334   Geneviève Bujold in *Anne of the Thousand Days,* 1969

335   Alec Guinness in *Cromwell,* 1970

336
Jaime de Mora y Aragon,
Maurice Denham,
Michael Jayston,
Laurence Olivier,
Harry Andrews, and
John Forbes-Robertson in
Nicholas and Alexandra,
1971

337
Maggie Smith in
Travels with My Aunt,
1972

338
Robert Redford
in *The Sting*,
1973

339
Robert Redford,
Mia Farrow in
The Great Gatsby,
1974

340   Ryan O'Neal, Marisa Berenson in *Barry Lyndon*, 1975

341   Donald Sutherland in *Il Casanova di Fellini*, 1976

342
Mark Hamill,
Harrison Ford,
Carrie Fisher
in *Star Wars*,
1977

343   Bette Davis in *Death on the Nile*, 1978

344   Sandahl Bergman in *All That Jazz*, 1979

345
Nastassia Kinski
in *Tess*, 1980

346
Alice Krige,
Ben Cross in
Chariots of Fire,
1981

347
Ben Kingsley
in *Gandhi*,
1982

348
Ewa Fröling in
Fanny och Alexander,
1983

349
Tom Hulce,
Elizabeth
Berridge
in *Amadeus*,
1984

350
Tatsuya
Nakadei
in *Ran*,
1985

351   Julian Sands, Helena Bonham-Carter in *A Room with a View*, 1986

352   Wu Chun Mei in *The Last Emperor*, 1987

353   Michelle Pfeiffer, John Malkovich in *Dangerous Liaisons*, 1988

354   Kenneth Branagh and Emma Thompson in *Henry V*, 1989

355   Anne Brochet, Vincent Perez, and Gérard Départieu in *Cyrano de Bergérac*, 1990

356
Annette Bening and
Warren Beatty in
Bugsy,
1991

357
Winona Ryder in
Bram Stoker's Dracula,
1992

358 Michelle Pfeiffer in *The Age of Innocence*, 1993

359
Terence Stamp
in *The Adventures of
Priscilla, Queen of
Desert,*
1994

360
Robert Downey Jr.
in *Restoration,*
1995

Catalogue Checklist

Where the names of the director or costume designer are not given, this information was not available.

Seven Decades of Fashion

The Twenties

1 Pola Negri, 1924

Pola Negri began working in 1917 in Germany under Max Reinhardt and Ernst Lubitsch and went to the United States in 1923, where she became one of the Hollywood silent-film queens. With her eccentric personality and spectacular love affairs she created a sensation. In 1929, when her star was beginning to wane, she went back to Germany, where she remained until the outbreak of the Second World War.

2 Mary Pickford and Katherine Griffith in *Pollyanna,* 1920
Directed by Paul Powell
Costumes by Walter Plunkett

Mary Pickford, America's sweetheart of the twenties, was typecast as a teenage Goldilocks for a long time. She was 27 when she played a twelve-year-old girl in *Pollyanna.*

3 Cullen Landis and Helene Costello in *The Lights of New York,* 1928
Directed by Brian Foy

Warner Brothers advertised *The Lights of New York* as 'the first 100% all-talking motion picture' and had an enormous box-office success.

4 Janet Gaynor and Charles Farrell in *Sunny Side Up,* 1927
Directed by David Butler
Costumes by Sophie Wachner

Janet Gaynor and Charles Farrell were 'America's favourite love birds' in the late twenties and early thirties. In 1927 Janet Gaynor was the first actress to be awarded an Oscar for Best Actress.

5 Gloria Swanson in *Sunset Boulevard,* 1950
Directed by Billy Wilder
Costumes by René Hubert

In *Sunset Boulevard* Gloria Swanson plays a former Hollywood silent-film star who keeps viewing her own old films to recreate her glamorous past. Extracts from these are included in the film, and our picture is from one of them.

6 Colleen Moore, the prototype of the twenties, with the director Mervyn LeRoy

7 Leslie Fenton and Madge Bellamy in *Black Paradise,* 1926

8 Mae Murray in *The Merry Widow,* 1925
Directed by Erich von Stroheim
Costumes by Adrian

The Merry Widow by Franz Lehár, directed by Erich von Stroheim for MGM, was the highlight in the career of Mae Murray, who was one of the greatest stars of the twenties. It was the first major film for which Adrian designed the costumes. His break with the traditional opera ballgown, which he replaced with a close-cut dress of worldly elegance, immediately established him in the front rank of the Hollywood costume world.

9 Jeanette MacDonald in the musical *Magic Ring,* 1929

Jeanette MacDonald played in several operettas and musicals as partner to Maurice Chevalier, and later with her regular partner Nelson Eddy.

10 Greta Garbo and Nils Asther in *The Single Standard,* 1929
Directed by John S. Robertson
Costumes by Adrian

Greta Garbo was Adrian's favorite star, and he designed the costumes for many of her famous historical films. Adrian left MGM and Hollywood when 'the divine Garbo' did. Our picture shows Greta Garbo in loose-fitting slacks, an unusually modern item of dress for the twenties.

11 Conrad Nagel and Greta Garbo in *The Mysterious Lady,* 1928
Directed by Fred Niblo
Costumes by Gilbert Clark

12 Greta Garbo and Jacques Feyder in *Anna Christie,* 1929
Directed by Clarence Brown
Costumes by Adrian

Greta Garbo is wearing a raincoat designed by Adrian, in which she created such a sensation that the designer seriously considered becoming a couturier; he did so in 1942.

13 Rita Cansino (Rita Hayworth) and Astrid Allwyn in *Dante's Inferno,* 1935
Directed by Harry Lachman
Costumes by Royer

Rita Cansino had a minor appearance in this, her first film, as a dark-haired dancer. It was to be the beginning of a great career as Rita Hayworth.

The Thirties

14 Gary Cooper, Claudette Colbert, and Ernst Lubitsch in *Bluebeard's Eighth Wife,* 1938
Directed by Ernst Lubitsch
Costumes by Travis Banton

Travis Banton created magnificent costumes for Claudette Colbert, one of the best-dressed women in films at the time. They were displayed to particular advantage in the elegant social comedies made by Ernst Lubitsch.

15 Greta Garbo and Melvyn Douglas in *Ninotchka,* 1939
Directed by Ernst Lubitsch
Costumes by Adrian

Adrian's designs for Greta Garbo played a great part in the plot of this film. They had to show how the Soviet woman commissar, with her strict ideological training, could fall victim to capitalism for a time and forget her political mission over an outrageous hat. Designing the sober working dress for Ninotchka was no doubt a particular challenge to Adrian.

16 Peggy Fears in *Lottery Lover,* 1935
Directed by William Thiele
Costumes by René Hubert, William Lambert

17 Clark Gable and Norma Shearer in *Idiot's Delight,* 1939
Directed by Clarence Brown
Costumes by Adrian

Clark Gable was in top form in this film, firmly establishing his image as a sovereign and ironic heartbreaker with enormous sensual appeal.

18 Clark Gable and Claudette Colbert in
It Happened One Night, 1934
Directed by Frank Capra
Costumes by Robert Kalloch

Frank Capra's film is regarded as the first 'screwball comedy' in the history of the cinema.

19 Lilian Harvey, 1934

Lilian Harvey, in Germany the regular partner of Willy Fritsch, had little success in Hollywood with her fresh and girlish charm.

20 Myrna Loy in
The Mask of Fu Manchu, 1930
Directed by Charles Brabin and King Vidor
Costumes by Adrian

21 *The Divorce of Lady X,* 1938
Directed by Tim Whelan
Costumes by René Hubert
Accessories for Merle Oberon

22 Laura Hope Crews and Marlene Dietrich in
Angel, 1937
Directed by Ernst Lubitsch
Costumes by Travis Banton

In *Angel* Marlene Dietrich was to personify the perfect lady, according to Ernst Lubitsch, and Travis Banton effectively underlined this with his costumes. Despite her faultless external appearance Marlene succeeded in imbuing the role with a touch of wickedness.

23 Marlene Dietrich and John Halliday in
Desire, 1936
Directed by Frank Borzage
Costumes by Travis Banton

In *Desire* Marlene Dietrich relaxed her icy image for the first time and was allowed to show some feeling.

24 Marlene Dietrich, 1934

Travis Banton designed Marlene Dietrich's private wardrobe as well. The man's suit, which she liked to wear particularly in the mid-thirties, aroused much attention. 'Marlene Dietrich slacks,' as they came to be known, are still fashionable today.

The Forties

25 Eve Arden, Jinx Falkenburg, Otto Kruger, and Anita Colby in
Cover Girl, 1944
Directed by Charles Vidor
Costumes by Travis Banton, Gwen Wakeling, and Muriel King

The forties were the richest decade in American film, as Hollywood fascinated the masses to distract them from the less pleasant reality of life. There was great demand for expensive but trivial productions that would easily attract an audience into the theaters in crowds. However, the costumes became simpler in keeping with the political and economic situation. *Cover Girl* was one of Rita Hayworth's greatest successes. In the film 15 delightful models represent the best-known magazines, from *Vogue* to *Cosmopolitan.*

26 Ann Sothern and Eleanor Powell in
Lady Be Good, 1941
Directed by Norman Z. McLeod
Costumes by Adrian

27 Hedy Lamarr, 1938

28 Anne Nagel and Constance Moore during a break in shooting, 1940

Anne Nagel and Constance Moore met on the set; Nagel was there for *A Modern Monte Christo,* Moore for *I'm Nobody's Sweetheart Now.*

29 Jean Rogers, 1940

30 Judy Garland, 1941

31 Paulette Goddard, 1941

Paulette Goddard was Charlie Chaplin's wife until 1942; she typified the capricious child-wife.

32 Bette Davis in
A Stolen Life, 1946
Directed by Curtis Bernhardt
Costumes by Orry-Kelly

Orry-Kelly created his finest gowns for Bette Davis. With great skill he used her figure to best advantage; through the use of specially designed corsets and expert garment cutting, she was made to more closely approximate the Hollywood image of beauty.

33 Lilli Palmer, 1947

34 Rona Anderson in
Floodtide, 1949
Directed by Frederick Wilson

35 Margaret Lockwood in
Bad Sister, 1947
Directed by Bernard Knowles

36 Ginger Rogers in
Lady in the Dark, 1944
Directed by Mitchell Leisen
Costumes by Edith Head, Raoul Pene du Bois, Mitchell Leisen, and Babs Wilometz

Ginger Rogers's costume for *Lady in the Dark* went down in cinematic history as the most expensive ever created. It cost (even then!) thirty-five thousand dollars, a sum which was worth much more in 1942 than it is today. It was created by the queen of designers, Edith Head, with bolero jacket and a wide skirt slit at the front, all out of mink. In the course of a dance number Ginger Rogers took off the jacket and opened the skirt, revealing tights and a lining in red and gold sequins. The effect was stupendous. But Edith Head was to learn in the same film that excessive expense could achieve exactly the opposite effect with the immense and elaborate wedding dress she also designed. It was so overdone, and Ginger Rogers looked so lost in it, that audiences laughed.

The Fifties

37, 39, 40 Audrey Hepburn in
Funny Face, 1957
Directed by Stanley Donen
Costumes by Edith Head, Hubert de Givenchy

Probably the best-known symbiosis between star and designer was that of Audrey Hepburn and Hubert de Givenchy, a relationship which Hepburn chronicles in her essay in this volume. In *Funny Face* Audrey Hepburn plays a girl who is discovered by a fashion photographer (Fred Astaire) and promotes a new line in fashion. In fact, with the help of Givenchy, who also dressed her in private life, Audrey Hepburn did create a completely new type of woman: cultured, restrained, and with youthful poise — a total contrast to the buxom beauties of the fifties.

38 Audrey Hepburn in
Roman Holiday, 1953
Directed by William Wyler
Costumes by Edith Head

See 'An Oscar for Costume Design' in this volume.

41 Mitzi Gaynor in
Anything Goes, 1956
Directed by Robert Lewis
Costumes by Edith Head

With his New Look Christian Dior created a new line — feminine, figure-revealing, and classically elegant, with the skirt at calf-length. The style, at which Edith Head was a master of definition, continued into the late fifties.

42 Sophia Loren in
Boy on a Dolphin, 1957
Directed by Jean Negulesco
Costumes by Anna Gobbi

43 Jayne Mansfield in
Will Success Spoil Rock Hunter?, 1957
Directed by Frank Tashlin
Costumes by Charles LeMaire

44 Joan Collins in
I Believe in You, 1952
Directed by Michael Relph, Basil
Dearden
Costumes by Anthony Mendleson

45 Marilyn Monroe and Tom Ewell in
The Seven Year Itch, 1955
Directed by Billy Wilder
Costumes by William Travilla

Travilla had a sure instinct for Marilyn
Monroe's individuality and knew how to
use her physical attractions to the very
best advantage, as he showed in films
like *Gentlemen Prefer Blondes, How to
Marry a Millionaire,* and *Bus Stop.*

46 Sophia Loren in
La Ciociara, 1960
Directed by Vittorio de Sica
Costumes by Ilio Costanzi

This was the greatest role of her career
for Sophia Loren, in a film for which she
won an Oscar. Reminiscent of the ex-
pressive force of Anna Magnani, her acting so complemented the neorealism of
Vittorio De Sica that one actually forgot
her beauty, as the *Sunday Times* put it.

47 Anita Ekberg, in
Artists and Models, 1955
Directed by Frank Tashlin
Costumes by Edith Head

48 Jack Palance and Corinne Calvert in
Flight to Tangier, 1953
Directed by Charles Marquis Warren

49 Marilyn Monroe in the fifties

50 Nadja Tiller in
Das Mädchen Rosemarie, 1958
Directed by Rolf Thiele
Costumes by Ursula Stutz

51 Elke Sommer in
Auf Wiedersehen, 1960
Directed by Harald Philipp
Costumes by Irma Pauli

The Sixties

52 Brigitte Bardot on the set for
La Vie privée, 1961

Directed by Louis Malle
Costumes by Marie-Martine Les Maisons
and Real

Brigitte Bardot was *the* idol for the
younger generation in the sixties. Countless girls wanted to look just like her — a
flowing, bohemian mane of hair, black
sloppy pullover, and tight jeans.

53 Brigitte Bardot in the sixties

In the Mary Quant look, wearing a wig.

54 Brigitte Bardot in
Les Novices, 1970
Directed by Guy Casaril
Costumes by Tatine Autre

55 Jacqueline Bisset in
Bullitt, 1968
Directed by Peter Yates
Costumes by Theodora Van Runkle

The sixties saw one of the greatest re-
volutions in fashion ever, as the scene
was overtaken by the hippy look — mini-
skirts, phosphorescent colors, glitzy
tights, and crocheted dresses; Carnaby
Street and ready-to-wear replaced haute
couture and Paris.

56 Raquel Welch in
Roustabout, 1964
Directed by John Rich
Costumes by Edith Head

The big costume departments gradually
became superfluous as, apart from historical films, commissions for costumes
increasingly went to independent
couturiers or costume designers. Edith
Head was one of the few leading costume
designers from Hollywood's great days
who continued the tradition. She won
her last Oscar in 1973.

57 Daliah Lavi and Laurence Harvey in
The Spy with a Cold Nose, 1966
Directed by Daniel Petrie
Costumes by Yvonne Blake

Daliah Lavi in the Courrèges look.

58 Glenna Forster-Jones and
Geneviève Waite in
Joanna, 1968
Directed by Michael Sarne
Costumes by Sue West

59 Marcello Mastroianni and
Sophia Loren in
La moglie del prete, 1970
Directed by Dino Risi
Costumes by Polidori, Mayer of Rome

The elegant, sophisticated Sophia Loren
in schoolgirl style.

60 Peter Sellers in
I Love You, Alice B. Toklas, 1968

Directed by Hy Averback
Costumes by Theodora Van Runkle

61 Natalie Wood and Ian Bannen in
Penelope, 1966
Directed by Arthur Hiller
Costumes by Edith Head

62 Barbra Streisand and Yves
Montand in
On a Clear Day You Can See Forever,
1970
Directed by Vincente Minnelli
Costumes by Cecil Beaton

63 Britt Ekland in
The Bobo, 1967
Directed by Robert Parrish
Costumes by Adriana Berselli

The Seventies

64 Charlotte Rampling in
La Chair de l'Orchidée, 1974
Directed by Patrice Chéreau
Costumes by Jacques Schmidt

65 Elke Sommer

Fashion in the seventies largely followed
the styles of the Swinging Sixties. The
Costume Look was still in. A clear sign of
the decline of the costume departments
came from MGM, which on the verge of
bankruptcy in 1969 auctioned off its entire stock of costumes. The libraries and
archives, until then maintained with lov-
ing care, suffered the same fate.

66 Ali MacGraw in
Love Story, 1970
Directed by Arthur Hiller
Costumes by Alice Manougian Martin

67 Jodie Forster in
Taxi Driver, 1976
Directed by Martin Scorsese
Costumes by Ruth Morley

In Martin Scorsese's award-winning film
Jodie Foster plays a teenage prostitute.
Her costume shows the gulf between the
realism of *Taxi Driver* and the usual
stereotyped images of prostitutes, as appeared in *Irma La Douce.*

68 Audrey Hepburn in
Bloodline, 1979
Directed by Terence Young
Costumes by Enrico Sabbatini

Enrico Sabbatini was one of the leading
costume designers in American film.
Most recently his costumes for *Old Grin-
go* (1989) have aroused much attention.

69   Barbra Streisand in
A Star Is Born, 1976
Directed by Frank Pierson
Costumes by Shirley Strahm

Barbra Streisand in the Afro look.

The Eighties

70   Madonna in
Who's That Girl?, 1987
Directed by James Foley
Costumes by Deborah Lynn Scott

Madonna has had an enormous influence on fashion for the young. Her dress is always idiosyncratic, extreme, sexy, a style that plays ironically on the myth of Marilyn Monroe.

71   Melanie Griffith in
Something Wild, 1987
Directed by Jonathan Demme
Costumes by Eugenie Bafaloukas

Melanie Griffith's voodoo outfit in *Something Wild* is costuming in the dual sense, for the exotic urbane Lulu, whom she portrays in the film, is really a blonde country girl called Audrey who assumes the disguise in order to lead a wild life.

72   Chloe Webb and Gary Oldmann in
Sid and Nancy, 1986
Directed by Alex Cox
Costumes by Cathy Cook and Theda de Ramus

Dog collars, barbed wire, razor blades, bicycle chains, and other such implements are the accoutrements of Punk. *Sid and Nancy* tells the true story of Sid Vicious, bass player in the Sex Pistols, the most famous if not notorious Punk band in England. In 1978 Nancy's body was found in the Chelsea Hotel in New York, and Sid was accused of her murder. Before the trial took place he died of an overdose of drugs.

73   Bernadette Peters
and Mercedes Ruehl in
Slaves of New York, 1989
Directed by James Ivory
Costumes by Carol Ramsey and Stephen Sprouse

Stephen Sprouse, who designed the costumes for the fashion show in this film, is one of New York's leading young designers. An all-around artist, he has worked closely with Andy Warhol, Keith Haring, and Kenny Scharf. His costume and jewelery designs are greatly influenced by contemporary painting and by the Heavy Metal and Punk subculture and

his unconventional fashion shows have become a spectacular addition to New York's cultural scene.

74   Isabelle Adjani in
Mortelle Randonnée, 1983
Directed by Claude Miller
Costumes by Emilie Poirot and Renée Renard

The new sobriety of the career girl had made fashionable severely classical outfits — understatement in cashmere, silk, and other expensive fabrics.

75   Diane Keaton in
Baby Boom, 1987
Directed by Charles Shyer
Costumes by Susan Becker
Cerruti 1881 Femme

J.C. Wiatt, played by Diane Keaton, is the typical career woman of the 1980s, equipped with all the insignia of the yuppie culture — elegant understatement, menswear by leading designers. The costumes for *Baby Boom* are by leading designer Nino Cerruti.

76   Kelly McGillis in
Top Gun, 1986
Directed by Tony Scott
Costumes by Bobbie Read

77   Cher in 1986

... and the Nineties

78   Helen Mirren in
The Cook, the Thief, His Wife and Her Lover, 1989
Directed by Peter Greenaway
Costumes by Jean-Paul Gaultier

Jean-Paul Gaultier, enfant terrible of the Paris fashion world, designed the extravagant costumes of this film by Peter Greenaway, an outstanding example of a congenial partnership between author/director and couturier. Using almost only red and black, Gaultier has transmuted the ambivalent theme of the film, love and death, into a basic symbolic language.
(Photo: Pandis/Sygma)

79   *Aufzeichnungen zu Kleidern und Städten,* 1989
Directed by Wim Wenders

In this recent experimental documentary, Wim Wenders explores a hitherto neglected aspect of film and fashion. Comparing his own work with that of the fashion designer Yohji Yamamoto he discovers surprising parallels. The photo

shows the hands of Yamamoto and his staff altering a pattern. The sketch by Yamamoto signals the style of the nineties.
(Photo: Road Movies GmbH)

Trend-Setting Films

80   Mia Farrow and Robert Redford in
The Great Gatsby, 1974
Directed by Jack Clayton
Costumes by Theoni V. Aldredge,
Ralph Lauren

Nostalgic costume films were among the most successful in the seventies, and they also became trend-setters. One was *The Great Gatsby* from the novel by F. Scott Fitzgerald, set in the twenties (see also 'An Oscar for Costume Design' in this volume). Mia Farrow's costumes were designed by Theoni V. Aldredge, who was awarded an Oscar for them in 1974. Robert Redford's suits were by Ralph Lauren.

81   Claude Rains, Paul Henreid, Humphrey Bogart, Ingrid Bergman in
Casablanca, 1943
Directed by Michael Curtiz
Costumes by Orry-Kelly

Humphrey Bogart made the trench coat a classic in *Casablanca,* which became a cult film.

82   James Dean in
Rebel without a Cause, 1955
Directed by Nicholas Ray
Costumes by Moss Mabry

James Dean, who made only three films but became the idol of generations, embodied the young rebel (as Marlon Brando did in his early years). *Rebel without a Cause* made jeans, a white T-shirt, and windbreaker the indispensables of Bad-Boy fashion.

83   Jean-Paul Belmondo and
Jean Seberg in
A bout de souffle, 1959
Directed by Jean-Luc Godard

Jean-Luc Godard was one of the leading members of the *Nouvelle Vague,* a group of young French directors who emerged at the end of the fifties. Their films, distinguished by a highly personal, raw style, had a major influence on generations of filmmakers. *A bout de souffle* is still a cult film. Jean Seberg's uncompromisingly short hairstyle was imitated by countless self-assured young girls.

84   Brigitte Bardot in
Et Dieu créa la femme, 1956
Directed by Roger Vadim

Brigitte Bardot, very much with the help of the man who discovered her and became her first husband, Roger Vadim, created a new type of woman, one who openly displayed her femininity, with tight-fitting pullovers and a billowing mane of blonde hair. *Et Dieu créa la femme*, which was directed by Roger Vadim, was BB's breakthrough.

85   Audrey Hepburn in
Breakfast at Tiffany's, 1960
Directed by Blake Edwards
Costumes by Edith Head

Audrey Hepburn displayed all the fashion ingredients of the worldly woman of the sixties in this film.

86   Robert Shaw, Robert Redford, and Paul Newman in
The Sting, 1974
Directed by George Roy Hill
Costumes by Edith Head

Men's fashion was inspired by two cult films set in the thirties, *The Sting* and *Bonnie and Clyde*. Vests, pinstripes, and wide trousers came back into fashion.

87   Meryl Streep in
Out of Africa, 1986
Directed by Sydney Pollack
Costumes by Milena Canonero

Out of Africa created the Safari look for eager fashion hunters, and sand-colored, loose-fitting blouses and trousers became hits.

88   Warren Beatty and Faye Dunaway in
Bonnie and Clyde, 1967
Directed by Arthur Penn
Costumes by Theodora Van Runkle

When Faye Dunaway wore a beret in *Bonnie and Clyde*, production of the French item doubled.

89   Laura del Sol and Antonio Gades in
Carmen, 1983
Directed by Carlos Saura
Costumes by Teresa Nieto

Most of Carlos Saura's version of Bizet's opera *Carmen* was danced. Largely through the flamenco star in the film, Antonio Gades, the film created a fever for flamenco, which the dance schools gladly satisfied. Fashion designers also profited, as full skirts and leotards became part of the *Carmen* boom.

90   Madonna in
Desperately Seeking Susan, 1985
Directed by Susan Seidelman
Costumes by Loquasto

Madonna is one of the many Pop stars whose individual style has had a growing influence on teenage fashion in recent decades. Films have greatly contributed to this, particularly this one, directed by Susan Seidelman.

Hats

91   Irene in
the costume department at MGM

Irene, whose elegant style was also eagerly sought after by film stars in private life, was under contract as head costume designer to MGM from 1942 to 1949.

92   Gloria Swanson in
Sunset Boulevard, 1950
Directed by Billy Wilder
Costumes by René Hubert

Sunset Boulevard includes numerous extracts from Gloria Swanson's old films. Our picture is from the twenties.

93   Asta Nielsen in
Erdgeist, 1923
Directed by Leopold Jessner

Asta Nielsen was one of the great silent-film stars in Germany. Her film career ended when talkies began.

94   Jeanette MacDonald in the twenties

95   Greta Garbo in
Mata Hari, 1931
Directed by George Fitzmaurice
Costumes by Adrian

The dancer Mata Hari, played here by Greta Garbo, was arrested in 1917 on suspicion of being a spy and executed.

96   Greta Garbo in
The Painted Veil, 1934
Directed by Richard Boleslawski
Costumes by Adrian

97   Marlene Dietrich in
The Lady is Willing, 1942
Directed by Mitchell Leisen
Costumes by Irene

98   Zarah Leander in
La Habanera, 1937
Directed by Detlef Sierck (Douglas Sirk)

La Habanera was Zarah Leander's second film for Ufa (Berlin). In it she plays a Swedish woman who falls in love with a wealthy bullfighter in Puerto Rico and marries him. Her costumes are appropriately luxurious.

99   Hedy Lamarr in
Dishonored Lady, 1947

100   Dorothy Lovett in
Powder Town, 1942
Directed by Rowland V. Lee

101   Ruth Warrick in
Arch of Triumph, 1948
Directed by Lewis Milestone

102   Greer Garson in
Random Harvest, 1942
Directed by Mervyn LeRoy
Costumes by Robert Kalloch

103   Myrna Loy, known as 'Mrs. Thin Man' after her very successful *Thin Man* films, is seen here in a sombrero with turned-up brim (1940).

104   Patricia Morison in
The Roundup, 1941
Directed by Lesley Selander

105   Martha Vickers, 1946

106   Ann Sothern in
Gold Rush Maisie, 1940
Directed by Edwin L. Marin
Costumes by Dolly Tree

107   Dorothy Lamour in
My Favorite Brunette, 1947
Directed by Elliot Nugent

In a hat created by Josephi.

108   Joan Crawford, 1940

109   Rita Hayworth in
Tonight and Every Night, 1945
Directed by Victor Saville,
Costumes by Jean Louis and Marcel Vertes

110   Marlene Dietrich in
No Highway in the Sky, 1951
Directed by Henry Koster
Costumes by Christian Dior

In this film Dior was able to display his New Look on Marlene Dietrich. According to Thierry de Navacelle, she was 'the latest word in elegance' in the film.

111   Lauren Bacall in
The Big Sleep, 1946
Directed by Howard Hawks
Costumes by Leah Rhodes

The Big Sleep was the second film Lauren Bacall made with Humphrey Bogart. Like *The Maltese Falcon*, it was one of the film noir cult films.

112   Judy Garland in
For Me and My Gal, 1942
Directed by Busby Berkeley
Costumes by Robert Kalloch

113 Marguerite Chapman in
Mr. District Attorney, 1946
Directed by Robert B. Sinclair
Costumes by Jean Louis

The hats were by Kenneth Hopkins.

114 Merle Oberon in
Temptation, 1946
Directed by Irving Pichel
Costumes by Orry-Kelly

115 Gloria Swanson, 1941

116 Rosalind Russell in
Women, 1939
Directed by George Cukor
Costumes by Adrian

117 Ruth Warrick, 1941

Ruth Warrick, formerly a singer, had her
screen debut in 1941 with Orson Welles
in the classic *Citizen Kane*.

118 Loretta Young in
The Men in Her Life, 1941
Directed by Gregory Ratoff
Costumes by Charles LeMaire

The designer Charles LeMaire created
this elegant mink hat.

119 Sylvia Sidney in
The Searching Wind, 1946
Directed by William Dieterle
Costumes by Michael Woulfe, Dorothy
O'Hara

120 Olivia de Havilland in
Hold Back the Dawn, 1941
Directed by Mitchell Leisen
Costumes by Edith Head

121 Alec Guinness in
Kind Hearts and Coronets, 1949
Directed by Robert Hamer
Costumes by Anthony Mendleson

In this film Alec Guinness plays eight
members of an aristocratic family who
are murdered, one after another, by a
fanatic. Our picture shows him as one of
the women in the family.

122 Dolores del Rio in
Journey into Fear, 1942
Directed by Norman Forster
Costumes by Edward Stevenson

123 Deborah Kerr in the fifties

124 Jane Russell in
Son of Paleface, 1952
Directed by Frank Tashlin

125 Jean Seberg in
Bonjour Tristesse, 1958
Directed by Otto Preminger
Costumes by Hubert de Givenchy

126 Audrey Hepburn in
Funny Face, 1957
Directed by Stanley Donen
Costumes by Edith Head, Hubert
de Givenchy

127 Joan Collins in
I Believe in You, 1952
Directed by Michael Relph,
Basil Dearden
Costumes by Anthony Mendleson

128 Sophia Loren in
Arabesque, 1966
Directed by Stanley Donen
Costumes by Christian Dior

129 Audrey Hepburn in
How to Steal a Million, 1966
Directed by William Wyler
Costumes by Hubert de Givenchy

130 Shirley MacLaine in
What a Way to Go, 1964
Directed by J. Lee Thompson
Costumes by Edith Head, Moss Mabry

131 Ali MacGraw, 1971

132 Jane Fonda in
Klute, 1971
Directed by Alan J. Pakula
Costumes by Ann Roth

133 Brigitte Bardot in
L'Ours et la poupée, 1970
Directed by Michael Deville
Costumes by Gitt Magrini

Hair

134 Cliquot the poodle, Joan Crawford,
and Gertrude Wheeler during a break
in shooting
The Damned Don't Cry, 1950
Directed by Vincent Sherman
Costumes by Sheila O'Brian

135 Myrna Loy, 1936

136 Brigitte Helm in
Fürst Woronzeff, 1934
Directed by Arthur Robinson

Brigitte Helm was one of the most popular silent film stars in the twenties. She
became world-famous with her role as a
robot in Fritz Lang's *Metropolis*.

137 Merle Oberon in
Temptation, 1946
Directed by Irving Pichel
Costumes by Orry-Kelly

138 Virginia Mayo, 1954

139 Eleanor Parker, 1947

140 Paula Corday in
Too Young to Kiss, 1951
Directed by Robert Z. Leonard
Costumes by Helen Rose

141 Loretta Young in
The Men in Her Life, 1941
Directed by Gregory Ratoff
Costumes by Charles LeMaire

142 Rita Hayworth in
They Came to Cordura, 1959
Directed by Robert Rossen
Costumes by Tom Dawson, Jean Louis

After several of the lighting men in the
studio had said that Rita Hayworth's hair
looked like an ill-fitting wig, the star
changed her appearance at the beginning of the forties. The result: women
all over the world wanted to have
curly auburn hair.

143 Lilli Palmer, 1947

144 Rita Hayworth, 1946

145 John Wayne, Marlene Dietrich in
The Spoilers, 1942
Directed by Ray Enright
Costumes by Vera West

146 Elizabeth Taylor in
Rhapsody, 1954
Directed by Charles Vidor
Costumes by Helen Rose

147 Hildegard Knef in
Diplomatic Courier, 1952
Directed by Henry Hathaway
Costumes by Elois Jenssen

148 Audrey Hepburn 1953

149 Shirley MacLaine, 1960

150 Yves Montand, 1944

151 Elvis Presley, 1960

Elvis's hairstyle as much as his music
formed a whole generation. To look as
much like their idol as possible, young
men in the fifties put pounds of Brillcream on their hair.

152 Yul Brynner in
The Journey, 1959
Directed by Anatole Litvak
Costumes by René Hubert

153 Ali MacGraw in
Love Story, 1970
Directed by Arthur Hiller
Costumes by Alice Manougian Martin,
Pearl Somner

154   Isabelle Adjani in
Subway, 1985
Directed by Luc Besson

In *Subway* Isabelle Adjani plays the
bored wife of a rich businessman who
tries to get away from her middle-class
existence by delving into the Punk
world.

155   Marisa Berenson in
Barry Lyndon, 1975
Directed by Stanley Kubrick
Costumes by Ulla-Britt Søderlund,
Milena Canonero

Although the costumes and hairstyles in
Barry Lyndon look absolutely authentic,
the soft and often unpowdered hair of the
actors and actresses was not at all typical
of the eighteenth century.

156   Barbara Bach in
The Humanoid, 1979
Directed by George B. Lewis

The futuristic effects in this film are created not only with special effects and
strange costumes but also through the
hairstyles, which look like something
from another world.

157   Cher, 1986

This extravagant hairstyle astonished
Cher's audience in 1986.

Evening Dresses

158   Jane Russell in
The Revolt of Mamie Stover, 1956
Directed by Raoul Walsh
Costumes by William Travilla, Charles
LeMaire

William Travilla, who designed for Jane
Russell this tight-fitting dress with its
emphasis on the bosom, liked best to
work for Marilyn Monroe, who was originally intended to play Mamie Stover.

159   Mae West in
Every Day's a Holiday, 1938
Directed by A. Edward Sutherland
Costumes by Elsa Schiaparelli

Elsa Schiaparelli, who created Mae
West's extravagant wardrobe for this
film, refused to go to Hollywood for the
work on *Every Day's a Holiday* and fitted
the costumes on a tailor's dummy with
Mae West's measurements. The clothes
turned out to be too small for the star and
the costume department at Paramount
had to work feverishly to alter them. The
deal was certainly a good one for the Ita-

lian designer. She created a perfume
flask in Mae West's figure-of-eight out-
line and called it 'Shocking'.

160   Jeanette MacDonald in
The Firefly, 1937
Directed by Robert Z. Leonard
Costumes by Adrian

Jeanette MacDonald was one of the most
successful musical and operatic singers
in Hollywood in the thirties.

161   Clark Gable, Norma Shearer in
Idiot's Delight, 1939
Directed by Clarence Brown
Costumes by Adrian

162   Clark Gable, Jean Harlow in
Saratoga, 1937
Directed by Jack Conway
Costumes by Dolly Tree

Saratoga was Jean Harlow's last film.
Shortly after the shooting was finished
she died, at the age of only 26, of kidney
disease.

163   Barbara Stanwyck in a costume
designed by Edith Head (1940)

164   Olivia de Havilland in
The Male Animal, 1942
Directed by Elliot Nugent
Costumes by Howard Shoup

After leaving films Howard Shoup became the first president of the Costume
Designer Guild, from which he also
received the Adrian Award.

165   Hedy Lamarr in
Crossroads, 1942
Directed by Jack Conway
Costumes by Robert Kalloch

Robert Kalloch, who designed ballet
dresses for Anna Pavlova in his youth, is
regarded as the first really outstanding
designer at Columbia. His work was admired for its sophistication; Edith Head
once said of him: 'Banton is pure fashion,
Kalloch pure imagination.'

166   Carole Lombard in
To Be or Not to Be, 1942
Directed by Ernst Lubitsch
Costumes by Irene

This was one of Ernst Lubitsch's most
genial works, and his own way of settling
the score with the Nazi regime.

167   Annabella was the stage name of a
Frenchwoman who achieved great popu-
larity in her own country in the thirties
before going to Hollywood. However, she
was never really able to establish herself
there and after her divorce from Tyrone
Power in 1948 returned to Europe and
gave up acting altogether.

168   Marlene Dietrich in
Seven Sinners, 1940
Directed by Tay Garnett
Costumes by Irene

169   Marlene Dietrich in
The Devil Is a Woman, 1935
Directed by Josef von Sternberg
Costumes by Travis Banton

The Devil Is a Woman was Marlene Dietrich's last film with the director who discovered and promoted her, Josef von
Sternberg. She said it was also her favorite film, as she believed she looked her
best in it.

170   Marlene Dietrich in
A Foreign Affair, 1948
Directed by Billy Wilder
Costumes by Edith Head

171   Paulette Goddard, Joan Crawford,
Rosalind Russell, Norma Shearer,
Mary Boland in
The Women, 1939
Directed by George Cukor
Costumes by Adrian

172   Marguerite Chapman in
One Way to Love, 1946
Directed by Ray Enright
Costumes by Jean Louis

173   Joan Crawford in
Dancing Lady, 1933
Directed by Robert Z. Leonard
Costumes by Adrian

Joan Crawford plays a star, Janie Barlow,
in a creation of sequined chiffon by
Adrian. The dress, created especially for
the musical finale, cost five thousand dollars but was only on the screen for ten
seconds.

174   Sylvia Sidney in
Blood on the Sun, 1945
Directed by Frank Lloyd
Costumes by Robert Martien

175   Myrna Loy in
Evelyn Prentice, 1934
Directed by William K. Howard
Costumes by Dolly Tree

Myrna Loy's costume for this exotic and
romantic drama of India was inspired by
the calla lily.

176   Claudette Colbert in
The Palm Beach Story, 1942
Directed by Preston Sturges
Costumes by Irene

Irene's costumes for Claudette Colbert in
this film were among the most admired
and successful in her entire career at
MGM.

177 Lilli Palmer in
Body and Soul, 1947
Directed by Robert Rossen
Costumes by René Hubert

178 Dorothy Lamour in a dress by
Edith Head, 1939

179 Ginger Rogers in
Magnificent Doll, 1946
Directed by Frank Borzage
Costumes by Travis Banton, Vera West

In this film Ginger Rogers plays Dolly
Madison, America's first 'First Lady.'
Based on the biography by Irving Stone,
the film was admired more for its costumes than anything else.

180 Maureen O'Hara in
How Green Was My Valley, 1942
Directed by John Ford
Costumes by Gwen Wakeling

Maureen O'Hara played the daughter of a
Welsh miner in this Oscar-winning film
by John Ford.

181 Joan Leslie in
Hollywood Canteen, 1944
Directed by Delmer Daves
Costumes by Milo Anderson

182 Loretta Young in
A Night to Remember, 1942
Directed by Richard Welles

183 Rita Hayworth in
Cover Girl, 1944
Directed by Charles Vidor
Costumes by Travis Banton,
Gwen Wakeling, Muriel King

184 Rita Hayworth in
Gilda, 1946
Directed by Charles Vidor
Costumes by Jean Louis

Gilda is certainly Rita Hayworth's most
famous film. A lasting influence on
cinematic musicals was made by the
scene in which she sings the legendary
number 'Put the Blame on Mame, Boys.'
For this number Jean Louis created a
tight black evening dress, slit to the thigh,
with matching long gloves that Rita Hayworth sensuously and provocatively
strips off and throws into the audience.

185 Suzy Parker, 1957

186 Anita Ekberg in
Artists and Models, 1955
Directed by Frank Tashlin
Costumes by Edith Head

187 Shirley MacLaine in
What a Way to Go!, 1964
Directed by J. Lee Thompson
Costumes by Edith Head, Moss Mabry

188 Elizabeth Taylor in
Elephant Walk, 1954
Directed by William Dieterle
Costumes by Edith Head

189 Elizabeth Taylor in
Julia Misbehaves, 1948
Directed by Jack Conway
Costumes by Irene

190 Marilyn Monroe in
All about Eve, 1950
Directed by Joseph L. Mankiewicz
Costumes by Edith Head

In *All about Eve* the young Marilyn Monroe plays a starlet who would do anything
for her career. It was her sixth film, and
her performance earned her a new contract with Fox.

191 Marilyn Monroe in
The Prince and the Showgirl, 1957
Directed by Laurence Olivier
Costumes by Beatrice Dawson

When MGM auctioned its stock of costumes in 1969, MM's evening dress for
this film achieved the highest price.

192 Pier Angeli in
The Flame and the Flesh, 1954
Directed by Richard Brooks

Pier Angeli, the prototype of the clean,
innocent girl, plays a rival to Lana
Turner in this remake of *Naples au baiser
du feu* of 1937.

193 Ann Todd in a dress by Glenny,
1948

194 Grace Kelly and Frank Sinatra in
High Society, 1956
Directed by Charles Walters
Costumes by Helen Rose

Helen Rose was the favorite costume designer of Grace Kelly, Lana Turner, and
Elizabeth Taylor. As a token of their esteem both Liz Taylor (for her wedding to
Nicky Hilton) and Grace Kelly were married in dresses designed by Helen Rose.
Liz Taylor wore an adaptation of the costume for *Father of the Bride* and Grace
Kelly a dress given to her by MGM (now in
the Philadelphia Museum of Art).

195 Grace Kelly in
Dial M for Murder, 1954
Directed by Alfred Hitchcock
Costumes by Moss Mabry

196 Ava Gardner at the premiere of
The Barefoot Contessa, 1954
Directed by Joseph L. Mankiewicz
Costumes by Fontana

The Barefoot Contessa was one of the
most successful films made with Ava
Gardner, who died on January 25, 1990.

197 Audrey Hepburn in
Funny Face, 1957
Directed by Stanley Donen
Costumes by Edith Head, Hubert
de Givenchy

198 Patricia Morison in
The Roundup, 1941
Directed by Lesley Selander

199 Jayne Mansfield and Tom Ewell in
The Girl Can't Help It, 1956
Directed by Frank Tashlin
Costumes by Charles LeMaire

For Jayne Mansfield's imitation of Monroe, Fox made a fairly generous costume
allowance: thirty-five thousand dollars
for 18 costumes.

200 Betty Grable in
How to Marry a Millionaire, 1953
Directed by Jean Negulesco
Costumes by William Travilla

This film offered plenty of opportunity for
fashion display, as the three main parts
for women were those of models in a
fashion salon (played by Betty Grable,
Marilyn Monroe, and Lauren Bacall).

201 Sabrina at Ascot, 1957

Sabrina was the stage name of a film and
theater actress, seen here on her way to
the races at Royal Ascot.

202 Elsa Martinelli, 1956

203 Deborah Kerr in
The King and I, 1956
Directed by Walter Lang
Costumes by Irene Sharaff

Irene Sharaff won an Oscar for her costumes in this film.

204 Audrey Hepburn in
Sabrina, 1954
Directed by Billy Wilder
Costumes by Edith Head and Hubert
de Givenchy

205 Tina Louise, 1959

Tina Louise, a former model and night-
club singer, appeared in a number of
American television series in the sixties.

206 Sophia Loren, 1958

Gloves

207 Gene Tierney, 1942

208 Susanna Foster, 1945

209 Irene Dunne in
Sweet Adeline, 1935
Directed by Mervyn LeRoy
Costumes by Orry-Kelly

210 Dorothy Shay in
Comin' Round The Mountain, 1951
Directed by Charles Lamont
Costumes by Rosemary Odell

Dorothy Shay had her screen debut with
the comic duo Abbott and Costello.

211 Vera Ellen, 1952

212 Carmen Miranda in
Something for the Boys, 1944
Directed by Lewis Seiler
Costumes by Kay Nelson, Yvonne Wood

213 Grace Kelly in
To Catch a Thief, 1955
Directed by Alfred Hitchcock
Costumes by Edith Head

Grace Kelly is seen here at the fancy-
dress ball where the thief is unmasked.

214 Grace Kelly in
Rear Window, 1954
Directed by Alfred Hitchcock
Costumes by Edith Head

In this film Grace Kelly, Hitchcock's favorite actress after *Dial M for Murder*, plays
the elegant fiancée of the photo reporter
L. B. Jeffries (James Stewart).

Men's Fashions

215 David Niven, 1935

216 Charles Ray in
The Girl I Loved, 1923

217 Errol Flynn in
The Charge of the Light Brigade, 1936
Directed by Michael Curtiz
Costumes by Milo Anderson

218 Henry Fonda in
I Met My Love Again, 1938
Directed by Arthur Ripley
Costumes by Helen Taylor

219 Alec Guinness in
Kind Hearts and Coronets, 1949
Directed by Robert Hamer
Costumes by Anthony Mendleson

220 Lewis Stone in the thirties

221 George Gobel and David Niven
during shooting for
The Birds and the Bees, 1956

Directed by Norman Taurog
Costumes by Edith Head

222 Walter Connolly, Guy Kibbee in
Lady for a Day, 1933
Directed by Frank Capra
Costumes by Robert Kalloch

223 Michael Trubshaw during shooting
for *Encore*, 1952
and David Niven during shooting for
Appointment with Venus, in Pinewood
Studios, England

224 Yves Montand, 1961

225 Walter Pidgeon, 1943

226 Jean Gabin in
La Bête humaine, 1938
Directed by Jean Renoir

227 Daniel Day Lewis in
A Room with a View, 1986
Directed by James Ivory
Costumes by Jenny Beavan, John Bright

A Room with a View won three Oscars.
The costumes, faithful to the period
and giving a lively impression of the turn
of the century, were particularly well
received by the jury (see 'An Oscar for
Costume Design', elsewhere in this
volume).

228 Jean Louis in the forties

The costume designer Jean Louis in front
of the camera for a change.

229 Tyrone Power, 1942

230 Clark Gable in
Any Number Can Play, 1949
Directed by Mervyn LeRoy

231 Humphrey Bogart, 1939

232 Dirk Bogarde, 1950

233 Ronald Reagan, 1947

234 Cary Grant, John Williams in
To Catch a Thief, 1955
Directed by Alfred Hitchcock
Costumes by Edith Head

235 Marlon Brando in
A Streetcar Named Desire, 1951
Directed by Elia Kazan
Costumes by Lucinda Ballard

236 Anthony Perkins in
The Actress, 1953
Directed by George Cukor
Costumes by Walter Plunkett

237 John Wayne, 1953

238 Paul Newman in
Somebody Up There Likes Me, 1956
Directed by Robert Wise

239 Burt Lancaster in
The Kentuckian, 1955
Directed by Burt Lancaster
Costumes by Norma

240 Richard Widmark in
The Law and Jake Wade, 1958
Directed by John Sturges
Costumes by Walter Plunkett

241 Ernest Borgnine in
The Catered Affair, 1956
Directed by Richard Brooks

242 Elvis Presley in
Flaming Star, 1960
Directed by Don Siegel
Costumes by Adele Balken

243 Director Fred Zinnemann (center)
visiting Marlon Brando (left) and Mont-
gomery Clift during the shooting for
The Young Lions, 1958
Directed by Edward Dmytryk
Costumes by Adele Balken, Charles
LeMaire

244 James Dean, Corey Allen in
Rebel without a Cause, 1955
Directed by Nicholas Ray
Costumes by Moss Mabry
(See 'Trend-Setting Films' elsewhere in
this volume.)

245 Jean-Paul Belmondo,
Jean Seberg in
A bout de souffle, 1959
Directed by Jean-Luc Godard

Belmondo imitates Bogie, but the small-
time *Nouvelle Vague* gangster on the run
is not a copy of the classic but a type in
his own right. Godard's film and
Belmondo's performance as Michel
Poiccard created a life style that went
beyond the fashion of the clothes.

246 Horst Buchholz in
Das Totenschiff, 1959
Directed by Georg Tressler

Horst Buchholz was regarded for many
years as the German James Dean, the
'angry young rebel' of Berlin.

247 Marlon Brando in
A Streetcar Named Desire, 1951
Directed by Elia Kazan
Costumes by Lucinda Ballard

Four years before James Dean made
casual wear top fashion in *Rebel without
a Cause*, Marlon Brando deliberately
moved away from the gentleman image

in *A Streetcar Named Desire.* The hard macho in a T-shirt was suddenly popular.

248 Marcello Mastroianni in
La dolce vita, 1961
Directed by Federico Fellini
Costumes by Piero Gherardi

(See 'An Oscar for Costume Design' elsewhere in this volume.)

249 Dennis Hopper, Peter Fonda in
Easy Rider, 1969
Directed by Dennis Hopper

Easy Rider has long been a cult film. The clothing worn by the male leads is in keeping with this — leather jackets, leather jeans, neckcloths.

250 *The Wanderers,* 1979
Directed by Philip Kaufman
Costumes by Robert de Mora

The Wanderers features a street gang in America in the sixties. Their clothing, like that of the Rockers, signals a cool strength.

251 Julie Christie, Warren Beatty in
Shampoo, 1975
Directed by Hal Ashby
Costumes by Anthea Sylbert

Warren Beatty in the role of the high-society hairdresser George in the typical seventies look.

252 Donald Sutherland in
Steelyard Blues, 1973
Directed by Alan Myerson

253 Scene from
Mad Max 2 — The Road Warrior, 1982
Directed by George Miller
Costumes by Norma Moriceau

The Punk wave (at the beginning of the eighties) clearly influenced the end-time movie. Two gangs in futuristic garb fight for the last drop of gasoline in a world devastated by the nuclear bomb.

254 Kevin Costner in
The Untouchables, 1987
Directed by Brian De Palma
Costumes by Marilyn Vance-Straker with Giorgio Armani

Armani designed a complete collection in the style of the thirties and so revived the Prohibition era in America.

255 Jack Nicholson in
The Witches of Eastwick, 1987
Directed by George Miller
Costumes by Aggie Guerard Rodgers with Cerruti 1881

Cerruti was responsible for the menswear in the film, and he designed this perfectly fitting dinner jacket for Jack Nicholson.

256 Arsenio Hall, Eddie Murphy in
Coming to America, 1988
Directed by John Landis
Costumes by Deborah Nadoolman

Deborah Nadoolman admits that she was inspired both by the Dior collections of the fifties and the everyday dress of the inhabitants of Senegal and the Ivory Coast.

Period Costumes

257 Hedy Lamarr in
Lady of the Tropics, 1939
Directed by Jack Conway
Costumes by Adrian, Valles

Hedy Lamarr's costume by Adrian is a mixture of Thai impressions, Hollywood fantasy, and oriental motifs.

258 Greta Garbo in
Camille, 1936
Directed by George Cukor
Costumes by Adrian

The costumes for Greta Garbo are among the most beautiful Adrian ever created. He showed a particularly fine sense of the subject in *Camille,* where the clothes became richer and more luxurious in the course of the action. His extravaganzas gave rise to numerous legends, and it was said in Hollywood that even Greta Garbo's underwear was handstitched for this film. When the shooting was finished, he gave his diva a pair of gloves in mauve glacé leather, with the initials GG embroidered in seed pearls on the cuffs.

259 Greta Garbo in
Queen Christina, 1933
Directed by Rouben Mamoulian
Costumes by Adrian

Adrian's costumes for *Queen Christina* imbued the whole film with quality. His designs only very slightly followed historical models; even the coronation robe for the Swedish queen was more like an evening dress of the thirties than a seventeenth-century robe of state. This was one of the reasons why the costumes were copied and sold well on Fifth Avenue.

260 Greta Garbo and Ramon Novarro in
Mata Hari, 1931

Directed by George Fitzmaurice
Costumes by Adrian

Adrian produced some of his most extravagant creations for Greta Garbo's role as Mata Hari, the dancer and spy, and after the shooting was finished the costumes were exhibited throughout America. One dance costume particularly, with a little embroidered Byzantine cap, made film and costume history (see also no. 95).

261 Greta Garbo in
Conquest, 1937
Directed by Clarence Brown
Costumes by Adrian

262 Greta Garbo and Fredric March in
Anna Karenina, 1935
Directed by Clarence Brown
Costumes by Adrian

For Tolstoy's tragic heroine Anna Karenina (whom Garbo had already portrayed in 1927 in a silent film), Adrian used miles of sheer tulle, his favorite fabric.

263 Greta Garbo and Robert Taylor in
Camille, 1936
Directed by George Cukor
Costumes by Adrian

Adrian devoted an unusual amount of attention in this film to the costumes for the male lead, Robert Taylor, and they are of an originality that would be hard to surpass.

264 Marlene Dietrich in
Kismet, 1944
Directed by William Dieterle
Costumes by Irene

265 Marlene Dietrich in
Golden Earrings, 1947
Directed by Mitchell Leisen
Costumes by Kay Dodson

When Marlene Dietrich agreed to accept the part of a gypsy, she went to study the gypsies living near Paris. She turned down the costumes created for her by Paramount on the grounds that they lacked authenticity, and changed them to what she thought was correct. She then used a dark brown makeup and made herself somewhat unpopular with her fans.

266 Marlene Dietrich in
The Scarlet Empress, 1934
Directed by Josef von Sternberg
Costumes by Travis Banton

For Marlene Dietrich's role as the czarina, Travis Banton created some of his most beautiful and magnificent costumes, again barely having any relation to historical models.

267 Marlene Dietrich in
The Scarlet Empress, 1934
Directed by Josef von Sternberg
Costumes by Travis Banton

At the behest of the head of Paramount, Adolph Zukor, Travis Banton wrapped Marlene Dietrich and the other members of the cast of this film in opulent furs. Zukor had been a furrier, and he was hoping to give the fur trade a boost.

268 Marlene Dietrich in
The Scarlet Empress, 1934
Directed by Josef von Sternberg
Costumes by Travis Banton

Travis Banton, who also designed men's suits for the private life of his favorite star, Marlene Dietrich, actually put her in hussar's uniform as Empress of Russia.

269 Marlene Dietrich in
The Scarlet Empress, 1934
Directed by Josef von Sternberg
Costumes by Travis Banton

It is partly thanks to Travis Banton's costumes for Marlene Dietrich that Josef von Sternberg's version has gone down in cinema history as the finest film on Catherine the Great.

270 Pola Negri and Rod La Rocque in
Forbidden Paradise, 1924
Directed by Ernst Lubitsch
Costumes by Howard Greer

Howard Greer's career in Hollywood began with his designs for Pola Negri in her first American film, *The Spanish Dancer,* 1923. 'La Negri,' as the demanding star was called, was very pleased with Greer's work, for he plied her with pearls, jewels, and lace, as we see here in *Forbidden Paradise,* where she plays Catherine the Great.

271 Joan Gardner and
Douglas Fairbanks Jr. in
Catherine the Great, 1934
Directed by Paul Czinner
Costumes by John Armstrong

Elisabeth Bergner, who emigrated to England in 1933, played the title role in the British film of *Catherine the Great* under the direction of her husband, Paul Czinner.

272 Brigitte Horney in
Münchhausen, 1942
Directed by Josef von Baky
Costumes by Manon Hahn

Brigitte Horney as Catherine the Great in the legendary *Münchhausen* film, with Hans Albers in the title role.

273 Tallulah Bankhead in
A Royal Scandal, 1945

Directed by Otto Preminger
Costumes by René Hubert

Tallulah Bankhead was known mainly as a stage actress, but moviegoers will remember her from Hitchcock's *Lifeboat.*

274 Peter O'Toole and
Jeanne Moreau in
Great Catherine, 1968
Directed by Gordon Flemyng
Costumes by Margaret Furse

Gordon Flemyng's film about the Russian Empress (from the stage play by George Bernard Shaw) is an opulent costume film. Peter O'Toole, who not only played the male lead but also produced the film, succeeded in borrowing the real crown jewels of the Romanovs for Jeanne Moreau.

275 Theda Bara in
Cleopatra, 1917

Theda Bara went down in film history as the first screen Cleopatra. Between 1914 and 1919 she acted in more than 40 silent films that won her renown as 'The Vamp.' 'Kiss me, my fool!,' the subtitle of her first great film, became a popular saying.

276 Claudette Colbert in
Cleopatra, 1934
Directed by Cecil B. DeMille
Costumes by Travis Banton

Cecil B. DeMille's version of *Cleopatra* is held to be the most entrancing visually. The costumes and settings are a mix of Art Deco and Egyptian ornamentation, while Claudette Colbert's hairstyle, which she also wore in another film of 1934, *It Happened One Night,* became her personal insignia and the current fashion.

277 Rhonda Fleming in
Serpent of the Nile, 1953
Directed by William Castle
Costumes by Jean Louis

278 Elizabeth Taylor and Rex
Harrison in
Cleopatra, 1963
Directed by Joseph L. Mankiewicz
Costumes by Irene Sharaff, Vittorio Nino Novarese

Elizabeth Taylor's costumes were discussed heatedly in the press when the film appeared, as too little attention had been paid to historical models and much more to the fashion of the sixties for emphasizing the figure. Irene Sharaff, who also designed Liz Taylor's costumes for *The Taming of the Shrew* and *Who's Afraid of Virginia Woolf?,* won an Oscar for *Cleopatra* (see 'An Oscar for Costume Design' elsewhere in this volume).

279 Vivien Leigh and Flora Robson in
Caesar and Cleopatra, 1946
Directed by Gabriel Pascal
Costumes by Oliver Messel

Oliver Messel, a highly gifted costume designer in the theater, worked for films as well from 1943 to 1948.

280 Gaby Morlay in
Entente cordiale, 1939
Directed by Marcel L'Herbier
Costumes by Boris Bilinsky

Gaby Morlay was the popular star of numerous French silent films. Later she became a sensitive character actress, usually cast in the role of a mother.

281 Irene Dunne in
The Mudlark, 1950
Directed by Jean Negulesco
Costumes by Edward Stevenson,
Margaret Furse

Margaret Furse, who designed the costumes for a large number of historical films, was nominated for an Oscar for this film, together with Stevenson.

282, 283 Anton Walbrook
(Adolf Wohlbrück) and Anna Neagle in
Victoria the Great, 1937
Directed by Herbert Wilcox

Wilcox's film, which concentrates mainly on the private life of Queen Victoria and Prince Albert, was continued the following year in *Sixty Glorious Years,* with the same cast. Anna Neagle's costumes were copies of the authentic dresses owned by Queen Victoria which are now in the British Museum.

284 Gabriel Gabrio and
Edwige Feuillère in
Lucrezia Borgia, 1937
Directed by Abel Gance
Costumes by Granier, Bétout

This film about the life of Lucrezia Borgia (1480–1519), daughter of the Pope, was made by the French director Abel Gance, who became famous for his silent film *Napoléon,* made between 1925 and 1927.

285 Dick Powell and
Olivia de Havilland in
A Midsummer Night's Dream, 1935
Directed by Max Reinhardt, William Dieterle
Costumes by Max Bee

Warner Brothers astonished Hollywood by suddenly turning to classical literature and commissioning a German theater director for a play by Shakespeare. The legendary Max Reinhardt, who had already produced *A Midsummer Night's*

Dream in a number of European theaters, had emigrated from Germany in 1933.

286 Gladys George and Joseph Schildkraut in
Marie Antoinette, 1938
Directed by W. S. Van Dyke II
Costumes by Adrian, Gile Steele

For this film Adrian created some of his finest and most expensive costumes, which took three years to complete. A team of researchers required several months simply to find old prints, drawings, and antiques in Europe (see no. 287).

287 Scene from
Marie Antoinette, 1938
Directed by W. S. Van Dyke II
Costumes by Adrian, Gile Steele

The luxurious settings and costumes for this film required huge quantities of fabric imported from all over Europe. In addition to the actors in leading and walk-on roles, a cast of 152 extras had to be dressed and fitted with wigs.

288 Scene from
Münchhausen, 1942
Directed by Josef von Baky
Costumes by Manon Hahn

(See no. 289.)

289 Hans Albers and
Hubert von Meyerinck in
Münchhausen, 1942
Directed by Josef von Baky
Costumes by Manon Hahn

Ufa wanted to make a monumental film to mark its twenty-fifth anniversary, a film such as Germany had never seen before. So while the red pencil went into action for almost every other production, no expense or quality was spared for *Münchhausen.* For two hours at least, the audience was to forget the war.

290 Mona Maris

291 Alice Faye in
In Old Chicago, 1938
Directed by Henry King, Robert Webb
Costumes by Royer

292 Merle Oberon in
A Night in Paradise, 1946
Directed by Arthur Lubin
Costumes by Travis Banton

For Merle Oberon's part as the Persian Princess Delarai, Travis Banton created extravagant, exotic costumes with such tight-fitting trousers that the star could only lie or stand in them. Travis Banton

was her favorite designer, and she had insisted that he design for *A Song To Remember* a year before.

293 Vivien Leigh and Clark Gable in
Gone with the Wind, 1939
Directed by Victor Fleming
Costumes by Walter Plunkett

Walter Plunkett reached the peak of his career with his costumes for *Gone With the Wind.* In particular, the dress that Scarlett O'Hara makes out of an old curtain and is wearing when Rhett Butler visits her created a sensation; it went down in costume history as the 'curtain dress.' Walter Plunkett would almost certainly have won an Oscar for his work if the award had been available in 1939, but the Oscar for Costume Design only commenced in 1948.

294 Ingrid Bergman in
Saratoga Trunk, 1945
Directed by Sam Wood
Costumes by Leah Rhodes

Ingrid Bergman's costumes were made on a small budget, partly from remnants. One dress was in a fabric that was very popular for kitchen curtains and tablecloths in the forties and fifties.

An Oscar for Costume Design

295 Costume designer Edith Head with her eight Oscars

296 Ingrid Bergman and José Ferrer in
Joan of Arc, 1948 (c)
Directed by Victor Fleming
Costumes by Dorothy Jeakins, Karinska

Karinska was so successful with her designs for Ingrid Bergman's costumes in *The House of Lady Alquist* that she was commissioned to design for *Joan of Arc* as well. Her costumes for the French country girl set new standards of authenticity for historical films. They were all individually hand-sewn in the manner of the fifteenth century.

297 Laurence Olivier and
Jean Simmons in
Hamlet, 1948 (b/w)
Directed by Laurence Olivier
Costumes by Roger K. Furse

Roger K. Furse, who worked in the theater in London from 1936 to 1939, also designed the costumes for Laurence Olivier's *Othello.*

298 Olivia de Havilland and
Montgomery Clift in
The Heiress, 1949 (b/w)
Directed by William Wyler
Costumes by Edith Head, Gile Steele

Olivia de Havilland won a second Oscar for her part in this film, and Edith Head won the first of the eight she was to win.

299 Errol Flynn and Viveca Lindfors in
The Adventures of Don Juan, 1949 (c)
Directed by Vincent Sherman
Costumes by Leah Rhodes, William Travilla, Marjorie Best

William Travilla was only included in the preparatory work when Errol Flynn refused to war short puffed breeches and a ruff. Travilla altered the costumes to his satisfaction; although they were no longer exactly in keeping with the Renaissance style, they still looked credible.

300 Anne Baxter, Bette Davis,
Marilyn Monroe, and George Sanders in
All about Eve, 1950 (b/w)
Directed by Joseph L. Mankiewicz
Costumes by Edith Head, Charles LeMaire

Bette Davis's costumes were by Edith Head, the others by Charles LeMaire. Her evening gown for the party scene was only finished the night before the scene was to be shot. There had been no time for fittings and it did not fit. However she liked it because it was too big.

301 Hedy Lamarr and Victor Mature in
Samson and Delilah, 1950 (c)
Directed by Cecil B. DeMille
Costumes by Edith Head, Dorothy Jeakins, Elois Jenssen, Gile Steele, Gwen Wakeling

To create as opulent an ambience as possible, the designers borrowed from nomadic, Turkish, and Indian dress, although this was hardly in keeping with the Old Testament figure of Delilah. Edith Head won an Oscar for black-and-white design this year and another for color (see 'An Oscar for Costume Design' elsewhere in this volume).

302 Elizabeth Taylor
and Montgomery Clift in
A Place in the Sun, 1951 (b/w)
Directed by George Stevens
Costumes by Edith Head

Elizabeth Taylor's strapless evening dress in this film became a bestseller in the summer of 1951.

303 Gene Kelly and Leslie Caron in
An American in Paris, 1951 (c)

Directed by Vincente Minnelli
Costumes by Orry-Kelly, Walter Plunkett, Irene Sharaff

The most famous ballet scene in the film, for which 500 costumes had to be made, took twenty minutes. It incorporated well-known motifs from Dufy, Rousseau, and Renoir. The critics made particular mention of the costumes that Irene Sharaff designed from a picture by Toulouse-Lautrec for a Paris street scene in the film.

304   Lana Turner and Kirk Douglas in
The Bad and the Beautiful, 1952 (b/w)
Directed by Vincente Minnelli
Costumes by Helen Rose

Helen Rose used white chiffon and white fox for the first time in this film; later they were to be her specialty. *The Bad and the Beautiful* is regarded as a classic among films dealing with Hollywood itself.

305   José Ferrer and Zsa Zsa Gabor in
Moulin Rouge, 1952 (c)
Directed by John Huston
Costumes by Marcel Vertes, Elsa Schiaparelli

306   Gregory Peck, Eddi Albert, and Audrey Hepburn in
Roman Holiday, 1953 (b/w)
Directed by William Wyler
Costumes by Edith Head

307   Jean Simmons and
Richard Burton in
The Robe, 1953 (c)
Directed by Henry Koster
Costumes by Charles LeMaire, Emile Santiago

Since the film was originally to be made in black and white, many of the costumes had to be changed or bleached when the decision was made to film in color. Great attention was paid to detail, and the costumes sewn by machine often had to be subsequently altered by hand.

308   Humphrey Bogart,
Audrey Hepburn, and William Holden in
Sabrina, 1954 (b/w)
Directed by Billy Wilder
Costumes by Edith Head and Hubert de Givenchy

The flat shoes and tight-fitting torero trousers that Audrey Hepburn wore in this film became very fashionable.

309   Kazuo Hasegawa and Machiko Kyo in
Jigokumon, 1954 (c)
Directed by Teinosuke Kinugasa
Costumes by Sanzo Wada

310   Susan Hayward in
I'll Cry Tomorrow, 1955 (b/w)
Directed by Daniel Mann
Costumes by Helen Rose

311   Jennifer Jones in
Love is a Many-Splendored Thing, 1955 (c)
Directed by Henry King
Costumes by Charles LeMaire

The costumes for this melodramatic love story started a trend for Far Eastern fashion.

312   Deborah Kerr und Yul Brynner in
The King and I, 1956 (c)
Directed by Walter Lang
Costumes by Irene Sharaff

The attraction of Irene Sharaff's costumes for *The King and I* was the contrast between the exotic clothes worn by the King, which were in heavy Thai silk, and the sober and modest attire of the English governess. Deborah Kerr had great difficulty coping with the hoop skirts. For the dance scene, in which she wears a wonderful satin dress, the hoop skirt had to be padded to prevent injury, but the effect was worth the effort, and the little teacher sways like a great tulip over the glittering dance floor.

313   Paul Douglas and Judy Holliday in
The Solid Gold Cadillac, 1956 (b/w)
Directed by Richard Quine
Costumes by Jean Louis

314   Kay Kendall, Mitzi Gaynor and Taina Elg in
Les Girls, 1957 (b/w)
Directed by George Cukor
Costumes by Orry-Kelly

315   Leslie Caron and Louis Jourdan in
Gigi, 1958 (c)
Directed by Vincente Minnelli
Costumes by Cecil Beaton

316   Jack Lemmon and Joe E. Brown in
Some Like It Hot, 1959 (b/w)
Directed by Billy Wilder
Costumes by Orry-Kelly

The evening dress worn by Marilyn Monroe to sing 'I'm Through with Love' was so transparent that Billy Wilder had to use very skillful lighting to keep the crucial parts of the body in the dark. Marilyn Monroe would have liked all her wardrobe in this film to be rather more daring, but Orry-Kelly was of the opinion that Sugar Kane was a girl who 'goes so far but no further.'

317   Charlton Heston and
Haya Harareet in
Ben Hur, 1959 (c)

Directed by William Wyler
Costumes by Elizabeth Haffenden

Elizabeth Haffenden studied the robes on Roman statues and antique depictions and adapted these to the Hollywood taste.

318   Kirk Douglas in
Spartacus, 1960 (c)
Directed by Stanley Kubrick
Costumes by Valles, Bill Thomas

319   Lucille Ball and Bob Hope in
The Facts of Life, 1960 (b/w)
Directed by Melvin Frank
Costumes by Edith Head and Edward Stevenson

The Facts of Life was Stevenson's last film. Lucille Ball said appreciatively of him that he was a master at achieving a great effect with small changes.

320   Marcello Mastroianni and
Nadia Gray in
La dolce vita, 1961 (b/w)
Directed by Federico Fellini
Costumes by Piero Gherardi

Piero Gherardi, originally an architect, worked in the late fifties and early sixties as both set and costume designer for Fellini. He twice won an Oscar for his film work (see no. 324).

321   Natalie Wood and Richard Beymer in
West Side Story, 1961 (c)
Directed by Robert Wise, Jerome Robbins
Costumes by Irene Sharaff

Irene Sharaff faced very particular requirements in this movie version of the Broadway musical. The costumes had to be attractive but credible, and the dancers had do be able to move easily in them. Stretch denim was used for the jeans worn by the street gangs, which looked faded and worn.

322   Bette Davis and Joan Crawford in
Whatever Happened to Baby Jane?, 1962 (b/w)
Directed by Robert Aldrich
Costumes by Norma Koch

323   Laurence Harvey in
The Wonderful World of the Brothers Grimm, 1962 (c)
Directed by George Pal, Henry Gevin
Costumes by Mary Wills

324   Claudia Cardinale in
Otto e mezzo, 1963 (b/w)
Directed by Federico Fellini
Costumes by Piero Gherardi

(See no. 320.)

325 Elizabeth Taylor in
Cleopatra, 1963 (c)
Directed by Joseph L. Mankiewicz
Costumes by Irene Sharaff, Vittorio Nino
Novarese

(See no. 278.)

326 Sue Lyon and Richard Burton in
The Night of the Iguana, 1964 (b/w)
Directed by John Huston
Costumes by Dorothy Jeakins

327 Audrey Hepburn in
My Fair Lady, 1964 (c)
Directed by George Cukor
Costumes by Cecil Beaton

Audrey Hepburn wears the most extravagant and famous costume in this film at the races at Ascot.

328 Laurence Harvey, Julie Christie
and Dirk Bogarde in
Darling, 1965 (b/w)
Directed by John Schlesinger
Costumes by Julie Harris

Julie Harris stepped in for another costume designer on this film and had only two weeks for her work. So she had no choice but to buy some of the clothes in boutiques. Despite that difficulty the costuming of this film was a sensational success, although Julie Harris never regarded her work for *Darling* as her best achievement.

329 Geraldine Chaplin and
Omar Sharif in
Doctor Zhivago, 1965 (c)
Directed by David Lean
Costumes by Phyllis Dalton

The costumes by the British designer Phyllis Dalton had a lasting influence on fashion in the sixties. In particular, the Russian winter coats worn by Omar Sharif were the sales hit of the 1965/66 winter in New York. Even the house of Dior was inspired by these models, while another fashion house produced a 'Caviar Collection.'

330 Elizabeth Taylor and
Richard Burton in
Who's Afraid of Virginia Woolf?,
1966 (b/w)
Directed by Mike Nichols
Costumes by Irene Sharaff

Irene Sharaff, who created the magnificent costumes for Elizabeth Taylor in *Cleopatra* and *The Taming of the Shrew,* proved in this film that a good designer can turn a beautiful woman into an aging, overweight slut with the appropriate costumes.

331 Robert Shaw in
A Man for All Seasons, 1966 (c)
Directed by Fred Zinnemann
Costumes by Elizabeth Haffenden, Joan
Bridge

332 Richard Harris, Vanessa Redgrave,
and Franco Nero in
Camelot, 1967
Directed by Joshua Cogan
Costumes by John Truscott

333 Leonard Whiting and
Olivia Hussey in
Romeo and Juliet, 1968
Directed by Franco Zeffirelli
Costumes by Danilo Donati

Danilo Donati closely followed the historical costumes of the Shakespeare era for this film.

334 Geneviève Bujold in
Anne of the Thousand Days, 1969
Directed by Charles Jarrott
Costumes by Margaret Furse

335 Alec Guinness in
Cromwell, 1970
Directed by Ken Hughes
Costumes by Vittorio Nino Novarese

Vittorio Nino Novarese shared the Oscar for *Cleopatra* with Irene Sharaff in 1963.

336 Jaime de Mora y Aragon, Maurice
Denham, Michael Jayston, Laurence
Olivier, Harry Andrews, and John
Forbes-Robertson in
Nicholas and Alexandra, 1971
Directed by Franklin J. Shaffner
Costumes by Yvonne Blake, Antonio
Castillo

Although there was much praise for the authenticity of the costumes, attentive critics objected that the royal children were wearing hats, which was an anachronism.

337 Maggie Smith in
Travels with My Aunt, 1972
Directed by George Cukor
Costumes by Anthony Powell

338 Robert Redford in
The Sting, 1973
Directed by George Roy Hill
Costumes by Edith Head

The thirties costumes for Robert Redford and Paul Newman had a strong influence on men's fashion in the seventies.

339 Robert Redford and Mia Farrow in
The Great Gatsby, 1974
Directed by Jack Clayton
Costumes by Theoni V. Aldredge

(See no. 80.)

340 Ryan O'Neal and Marisa
Berenson in
Barry Lyndon, 1975
Directed by Stanley Kubrick
Costumes by Ulla-Britt Søderlund,
Milena Canonero

All the costumes in this film are exact copies of eighteenth-century clothes. Kubrick had the research for this done in archives, libraries, and private collections in the Midlands in England. Many of the items were solicited through advertisement. Altogether, the preparation for and production of the costumes took eighteen months.

341 Donald Sutherland in
Il Casanova di Fellini, 1976
Directed by Federico Fellini
Costumes by Danilo Donati

Fellini's Casanova won Danilo Donati, the costume designer for *Romeo and Juliet,* his second Oscar.

342 Mark Hamill, Harrison Ford, and
Carrie Fisher in
Star Wars, 1977
Directed by George Lucas
Costumes by John Mollo

343 Bette Davis in
Death on the Nile, 1978
Directed by John Guillermin
Costumes by Anthony Powell

344 Sandahl Bergman in
All That Jazz, 1979
Directed by Bob Fosse
Costumes by Albert Wolsky

345 Nastassia Kinski in
Tess, 1980
Directed by Roman Polanski
Costumes by Anthony Powell

346 Alice Krige and Ben Cross in
Chariots of Fire, 1981
Directed by Hugh Hudson
Costumes by Milena Canonero

347 Ben Kingsley in
Gandhi, 1982
Directed by Richard Attenborough
Costumes by John Mollo, Bhanu Athaiya

348 Ewa Fröling in
Fanny och Alexander, 1983
Directed by Ingmar Bergman
Costumes by Marik Vos

349 Tom Hulce and
Elizabeth Berridge in
Amadeus, 1984
Directed by Miloš Forman
Costumes by Theodor Pistek

350 Tatsuya Nakadai in
Ran, 1985
Directed by Akira Kurosawa
Costumes by Emi Wada

For this film, which had a cast for more than a thousand (including extras). Kurosawa had all the costumes, right down to the authentic underwear, made by traditional methods. The items included 2,500 straw sandals and fourteen hundred suits of armor. All the work processes, from dyeing to weaving were carried out by hand. The production of a single Japanese brocade robe from sixteenth-century models took between three and four months, as up to sixty different colors were used. The production of all the costumes took nearly three years.

351 Julian Sands and
Helena Bonham-Carter in
A Room with a View, 1986
Directed by James Ivory
Costumes by Jenny Beavan and John Bright

352 Wu Chun Mei in
The Last Emperor, 1987
Directed by Bernardo Bertolucci
Costumes by James Acheson

(see number 353.)

Mainly Chinese seamstresses and art students were engaged to produce the numerous costumes, and for the large crowd scenes 300 Red Guards had their heads shaved and pigtails stuck on. Altogether *The Last Emperor* won nine Oscars.
(Photo: Jugendfilm/Basil Pao)

353 John Malkovich and
Michelle Pfeiffer in
Dangerous Liaisons, 1988
Directed by Stephen Frears
Costumes by James Acheson

James Acheson worked for television before he began to design costumes for Monty Python films. He was also costume designer for *Time Bandits*, *Brazil* and *Highlander*.

354 Kenneth Branagh and
Emma Thompson in
Henry V, 1989
Directed by Kenneth Branagh
Costumes by Phyllis Dalton

355 Anne Brochet, Vincent Perez,
Gérard Départdieu in
Cyrano de Bergérac, 1990
Directed by Jean-Paul Rappeneau
Costumes by Franca Squarciapino

356 Annette Bening and
Warren Beatty in
Bugsy, 1991
Directed by Barry Levinson
Costumes by Albert Wolksy

357 Winona Ryder in
Bram Stoker's Dracula, 1992
Directed by Francis Ford Coppola
Costumes by Eiko Ishioka

358 Michelle Pfeiffer in
The Age of Innocence, 1993
Directed by Martin Scorcese
Costumes by Gabriella Pescucci

359 Terence Stamp in
*The Adventures of Priscilla,
Queen of Desert*, 1994
Directed by Stephan Elliott
Costumes by Lizzy Gardiner

360 Robert Downey Jr. in
Restoration, 1995
Directed by Michael Hoffman
Costumes by James Acheson

Index

The numbers refer to page numbers

I. Actors

II. Costume Designers

III. Directors

IV. Film Titels